VEGETARIAN DINNER PARTIES

The complete guide to preparing and serving exciting dinner party meals.

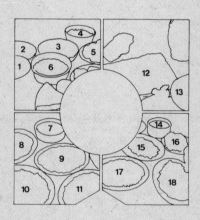

Recipes illustrated on cover:

1. Gratin Savoyard (page 94)
2. Tarte à l'Oignon Alsacienne (page 90)
3. Quiche Niçoise (page 88)
4. Haricots à la Charente (page 92)
5. Tomates Farcies Provençale (page 85)
6. Oignons à la Monégasque (page 91)
7. Dhall (page 26)
8. Rotis (page 35)
9. Pilau Rice (page 34)
10. Chick Pea Curry (page 28)
11. Vegetable Curry (page 30)
12. Pizza (page 50)
13. Lasagne al Forno (page 48)
14. Spicy Peanut Butter Sauce (page 124)
15. Stir-fried Vegetables (page 122)
16. Crispy Noodles with Ratatouille Sauce (page 127)
17. Fried Rice (page 125)
18. Fried Tofu (page 126)

VEGETARIAN DINNER PARTIES

by

LEON LEWIS

Illustrated by Clive Birch

THORSONS PUBLISHERS LIMITED
Wellingborough, Northamptonshire

First published 1983
Second Impression 1984

British Library Cataloguing in Publication Data

Lewis, Leon
  Vegetarian dinner parties.
  1. Vegetarian cookery
  I. Title
  641.5'636   TX837

ISBN 0-7225-0766-6

Printed and bound in Great Britain

CONTENTS

Wholefoods, quite simply, are foods in their natural state — nothing added, nothing taken away. In this age of mass-production foods, wholefoods are not always easy to obtain. But as nutritionalists and doctors become increasingly convinced of their value in building and maintaining health, so their availability is fast improving.

Include as many natural, unadulterated foods as you can in your day to day eating pattern, and discover not just exciting new tastes and a fresh approach to mealtimes, but better health too.

FOREWORD

In this book I have endeavoured to illustrate the ideas of vegetarian meal planning for both formal dinner parties of six to eight people and larger, less formal social evenings at which the meal plays a less prominent, but nonetheless important part of the proceedings. A flexible yet balanced structure of courses, different styles of cooking, as well as contrasts of colours, textures and flavours are all important on both such occasions. However, added interest can be given both to the host/hostess in his/her personal exploration of different styles of cooking, and to the discerning guest, by organizing these events around certain national or regional cookery traditions. This is an idea I have used successfully both in cooking for friends in my own home (and occasionally in theirs), and in catering at social evenings organized by the Vegetarian Society Youth Section in London.

This book is written in an effort to share the organizational trials and tribulations which may arise in attempting meals of such scale and scope, and also to share the culinary delights which hopefully result and which make the effort expended worth while.

In addition to introducing themes on which vegetarian gourmet food can be based, it is hoped that such a project will prove of some use in its own right.

INTRODUCTION

There are many limitations to consider in the preparation of any dinner party; the time available, the number of helpers you can enlist, the amount of cooker space, the area of working surfaces in your kitchen, the utensils available, facility for keeping cooked food warm and the amount of money you wish to spend. It is sensible, therefore, to consider carefully all of these aspects before embarking upon a dinner party so that you can determine the optimum number of guests and choice of menu for a perfect meal.

The time that must be allocated includes the planning of the menu, adaptation of recipes to suit personal tastes, the shopping, the enlistment of help, if necessary, and the actual preparation of the meal — not to mention the clearing up afterwards. It is hoped that the menus included in this book will be perfectly adequate but there is always the possibility of excluding certain dishes and including others (for example, where there is a need to use seasonal vegetables rather than ones that are unobtainable or expensive). Adaptation of recipes may be needed for similar reasons or because of personal taste — it is certainly wise to try out as many of the dishes as possible before attempting to put them together in the form of a dinner party.

While most chapters provide enough food and selection for a dinner party for up to twenty people, I have chosen various combinations of dishes and suggestions for smaller dinner parties of about six people when it is not practical to offer such a wide range of dishes. The chosen menus include starter, main course and dessert, although the lover of long feasts may extend the number of courses still further. Equally, there is considerable scope for varying each suggested menu by including dishes from elsewhere in the chapter, or even from other chapters. For instance, Mango Fool is a dessert which is excellent after any oriental meal; however, too random a selection of dishes from throughout the book is obviously unwise, as a meal of, say, Chow Mein, Pizza and Boxty Pancakes would be far from appetizing.

Many ingredients such as flour, dried beans, dried fruit, nuts, herbs and spices can be bought well in advance and will keep for a long time. Try to plan your shopping so that items such as vegetables and dairy produce are the only ones that have to be bought near the time of the party. There are many wholefood suppliers who will offer delivery and discount for large orders so do try to discover your local ones; market stalls dealing in wholefoods are good places at which to make enquiries. Many fruiterers will make an arrangement with you for supplying less common vegetables such as okra (ladies' fingers).

If you can persuade one or two of your friends to help you, this will make the meal preparation less tedious. These helpers should be enthusiastic and reliable, and if they will be eating the meal later on, their involvement in its preparation will stimulate their interest (and appetite). Cooking can be fun if a few like-minded people are happily engaged in the creation of a great meal, and there are several ways of making a good atmosphere even better, i.e. by offering drinks and playing some appropriate music so that cooking becomes a totally social experience and not a chore. The optimum number of helpers depends on the amount of work to be done in the time available and on the size of your cooking area. If each recipe has been carefully written out beforehand, each helper can have a recipe to which he or she can work and as long as all the ingredients and utensils are at hand, I find that this method works best of all.

Personal experience has led me to the realization that any enjoyable vegetarian meal can take one person several hours of preparation because of the many time-consuming processes involved. In their entirety, some of the meals in this book require the involvement of one or two helpers for about four hours, and while this may seem extravagant it is invariably better to have time to spare so that the presentation of the food can be given adequate care and attention.

It is also advisable to do as much washing up and clearing up as possible before the meal is served so that guests do not see the kitchen looking like a battlefield, and serving up is facilitated by having clean utensils and work surfaces available. Consideration must also be given to the layout of furniture, the laying of the table (or tables) and ensuring that all cutlery and crockery is spotless. Suitable drinks should be available for dispensing before the meal.

If there is no help available, then you could either prepare some of the dishes well in advance and use a deep-freeze, or do some of the dishes the previous day and store them in a refrigerator or cool place. (You should be in a condition to enjoy the meal when you come to eat it!)

Whether you have an electric or gas cooker, there is always a limit to the amount of food that can be cooked at any one time. Four rings is the usual number and so no more than four dishes can be prepared on the cooker-top at any one time. Furthermore, oven space is limited both by volume and by the number of shelves. As far as possible, the meals in this book have been designed to avoid too great a strain on the use of rings on the cooker-top and on oven space.

I personally prefer gas for cooker-top work because it is easier to ensure that you have the correct heat setting for any particular job. Both electric and gas ovens have their devotees; I believe that the most important consideration is to know your own oven, as there is significant variation in thermal efficiency and in the temperature of different parts of the oven. Be aware of the fact that regular opening and closing of the oven door will reduce the efficiency of your oven and yet, as far as possible, you should judge whether a dish is cooked to perfection by your own experience or expectation of its colour, smell and consistency, though there is no substitute for a taste test. If, for instance, two quiches of one type are to be cooked on two different shelves of your oven, you could change them over at half-time to that they are ready at about the same time.

Obviously, any cooked dishes that are served cold will be prepared first, generally followed by those with little or no vegetables, finishing with preparation of vegetable dishes and deep-frying where applicable. Some sort of time-table worked out in advance may be helpful, though after you have prepared four or five dinner parties you will have a feel of how the cooking is going.

There is often a natural break in the preparation of the various dishes when, for instance, all the dishes of one type have been prepared, and this can be an excellent opportunity to tidy up, replace ingredients and utensils which are no longer required, and find those ingredients and utensils which will be required. A certain amount of washing up can be done at this time and subsequently, so that a washing up 'mountain' is avoided. A dishwasher does have the advantage that when dirty utensils are no longer required they can immediately be stored out of your way in the machine until you have a full load. If no dishwasher is available, I highly recommend the installation and use of a double sink unit if you do not already have one.

You should ensure that an adequate number of chopping boards and sharp knives of an appropriate size are available as these will be needed sooner or later. Easy access to a waste bin is also a major priority — I abhor the cluttering up of sinks and working surfaces with peelings and other waste.

There are various 'gadgets' which ease the preparation of vegetarian meals, many of which are essential. Preference for different types of graters varies from person to person so I advise you only to be aware of the wide choice available. A garlic press is a great help, as are larger pepper mills and sea salt grinders. A rotary whisk has its uses, too.

Electrical gadgetry, however, is revolutionizing the modern kitchen. Machines that will chop, slice, grate, mince, blend and mix dough are well worth the investment. A coffee grinder is the best attachment for preparation of spice mixtures. Nuts are often better minced than ground and a grater attachment will give you the most useful option of finely grating them. A shredder is invaluable in making salads, and the blender in my kitchen is in constant use: for making smooth sauces, mayonnaise, *pâtés* such as hummus; for blending cream and egg mixtures for quiches, and for making fine breadcrumbs. Pastry can be made without any mess and other jobs can be done while it is being mixed. All cheese can be grated with minimal wastage, and even small vegetables such as sprouts are easily dealt with.

Because of constant changes in the price of ingredients (and especially local variation in prices), it is impossible to put an accurate figure on the cost of the ingredients, but I am convinced that the price of a gourmet vegetarian dinner party will always compare favourably with that of a similar dinner party which includes meat and fish.

While you are greeting guests and offering drinks, you may need to keep certain dishes warm. This is when there may be insufficient space in your oven. Warming drawers are included in most cookers; failing this, it might be an idea to invest in one of the convenient trolleys which are designed to keep food warm.

You can build up the guests' expectations of the meal by showing them the menu. Some of the meals include dishes which can be used as starters to be handed round with the drinks. A certain amount of 'education' of non-vegetarian guests may be possible at this stage, as they may have some ill-founded ideas about nutritional and other aspects of vegetarian food. These misconceptions can be corrected very swiftly. Do emphasize the health-giving aspects of vegetarian food; this might encourage smokers not to light up. I am personally convinced that the pursuit of health will lead many more people to become vegetarian in the future, though the humanitarian reasons for not rearing animals in a cruel way purely for human consumption are also most compelling. The display of cookery books, particularly ones with illustrations, is another excellent way to stimulate discussion and appetites.

There is no doubt that the appealing presentation of food is a determining factor in its acceptability particularly by non-vegetarians. Attractive serving bowls and the arrangement of food in them is essential. There are many ways of making your food more decorative. A chow mein, for example, topped with a dark-coloured mushroom sauce looks more tempting if sprinkled with a few chopped cashews. Useful garnishes include chopped nuts, sunflower seeds, tomato and lemon wedges, cress or parsley, peppers, fresh herbs and chives.

The number of guests and the size of your dining table will greatly influence whether you decide to serve the food as a buffet or at the table. Each method has its advantages. For a buffet you will need to have plates available at the start of the line. Dishes can be labelled and you can also supervise each person's own serving so that their questions about ingredients, method of cooking, etc., can be immediately answered. A buffet is usually more efficient in that all the serving is completed more quickly. A dining table can still be laid for use, or cutlery wrapped in serviettes can be made available at the end of the line if seating is more haphazard. One problem is that guests mislay their glasses while they are serving themselves and finding somewhere to sit and so it is advisable to appoint a drinks waiter whose job it will be to ensure that everyone has a drink to accompany their food. If you have a dining table large enough to accommodate all your guests, this will enable the meal to be enjoyed in a more formal and cosy atmosphere. You must ensure that every person has a chance to sample every dish. Therefore, it may be necessary to split up each dish into two or more serving bowls. Again, someone should be appointed to fill up glasses, as most tables will not accommodate bottles of wine as well as all the serving dishes and crockery.

Do remember that any left-overs can be used up at a later date if you have a freezer, as the majority of dishes in this book freeze well. If you gain as much pleasure from cooking and eating these meals as I have, you will be a very happy person.

1.

INDIA

In the same way that English cuisine does not consist entirely of stews, Indian food is not only curries. As you would expect of such a large country, there is wide variation in cooking styles, and there is also the possibility of experimentation with many different herbs and spices. Cooking in yogurt, with coconut or with tomato *purée* can also make interesting combinations of flavours.

There are several snacks that can be prepared as a starter to an Indian meal, but there are a number of reasons why it is not a good idea to provide more than two of these at one meal; they involve a lot of deep-frying and I am firmly against the consumption of too much fried food, particularly before a meal as, in excess, it dulls the appetite. Cooker space and time will also make it difficult to provide a complete selection; at least one person is needed to do the deep frying, and even a dozen onion *bhajis* takes twenty minutes. It is, of course, vital to have the fat at the correct temperature, and while ghee is recommended for frying by most Indian cooks, I find vegetable oil quite adequate and more convenient to use.

Spices should be bought whole where available and ground up only when required. Avoid buying large quantities of spices, and store them in air-tight jars. While it is traditional to pound the spice, it is more efficient to use an electric grinder. You will find all the spices mentioned easy to obtain in Indian shops and even supermarkets, so there is no need to buy made-up curry powder; also the proprietors of continental food shops are usually very willing to explain the use of the unfamiliar ingredients, and I take a delight in asking about every unfamiliar food on the shelves.

Some vegetables used in Indian cookery are unfamiliar to us but are becoming more widely available, both fresh and tinned. Where vegetables such as aubergines (eggplants) and *bhindis* are unavailable, you can simply substitute courgettes (zucchini) or green beans. Do try the unfamiliar vegetables such as *parwal* and *karela*, though be careful because *karela* is not called bitter gourd without reason.

Fresh chillis should be used in moderation, if at all. They are a most colourful addition to any dish but I must add a few words of warning: the smaller the chilli, the hotter it will be in general, and the puffy, often yellow peppers used in the West Indian chapter are by far the most powerful. The flesh of the chilli is milder than the pips so it is a good idea to use the top end of the chilli only. Do be careful not to rub your eyes after chopping the chillis as this will cause severe irritation. Cooked chillis are less 'powerful' than raw ones but cannot be used indiscriminately. It is far more sociable to provide a bowl of chopped raw chillis than to make unbearably hot dishes.

After planning the meal and buying the ingredients in the usual way, start the cooking of the meal by preparing ingredients which will be needed in several of the dishes, for instance onions, garlic and fresh coriander, as doing these jobs later will disturb the continuity of the cooking. It is quite possible to prepare three dishes simultaneously if all the small chores have been done and spices, grinders, knives, chopping boards etc. are at hand. Ingredients such as lentils, chick peas (garbanzo beans) and tamarind should ideally be soaked overnight, though a pressure cooker can be useful here. If fresh coconut is used, this must be broken, peeled and grated up in advance and this is a tiresome operation. It is easier to use desiccated or, preferably, creamed coconut.

Indian meals need much time and care in their preparation; allow at least four hours because a slow-cooked curry has an improved flavour. Indeed, it is often said that left-over curry, reheated next day, is the best of all.

Popadams of many flavours and sizes can be bought and fried, or even grilled, for eating before the main course is served. *Chura* (or *chevda*), and *sev* can be handed round in the same way that in England it is common to pass round peanuts to accompany aperitifs. *Chura* is a mixture of deep-fried chick peas (garbanzo beans), nuts and puffed rice. It is usually mixed with *sev*, which resembles vermicelli, and is made by deep-frying strands of spiced gram flour.

Fresh chutneys made from yogurt, cucumber, mint, coriander, and coconut, amongst many other ingredients, provide a welcome contrast to the pungency of the curry and no Indian meal is complete without them. Jars of chutney and pickles of many varieties can be purchased widely, and I like to provide a selection such as mango chutney, lime pickle, aubergine (eggplant) pickle and chilli pickle.

It is unwise to accompany curry with wine. Iced water or lager are undoubtedly the most suitable drinks to have with Indian food, though dry cider and fruit juice are possible alternatives.

The best of the white rices is basmati but, on nutritional grounds, I must advocate the use of long-grained brown rice. The vitamin content of brown rice is much higher than that of white rice because of the outer brown husk which contains vitamin B and which is not removed through polishing.

The choice of suitable menus for smaller dinner parties is quite simple as either the *pakoras* or onion *bhajis* can be omitted, and the following curries could be omitted: *dhall* or tomato, chick pea (garbanzo bean) or peanut. The vegetable curry need not be a mixed vegetable dish, and separate potato and cauliflower curries, for instance, may take its place. Rarely will you want to provide both *rotis* and rice and the range of chutneys and pickles that you prepare will depend on the time you have available and the grandeur of the meal.

As you become more adept, you will expand your range of dishes by improvisation (certainly the best way, though cookery books are useful for ideas), and find you are able to cope with even more elaborate menus. In fact, when you have completed the cooking of a curry, it can be kept in a low oven or warming drawer as long as it is covered and 'freshened' just before serving. This is advisable, and probably necessary, as most likely you will require the rings on your cooker-top for deep-frying the *bhajis* or *pakoras*.

Ingredients Used in Indian Cookery
Indian names are given in brackets.

Cardamom (*elaichi*) — there are three varieties commonly available: black, green and white. They are a member of the ginger family but are not hot like ginger itself. Use the softer and slightly larger white husk in desserts, discarding the outside pod and using the black seeds crushed. The harder, light green husk can be used in savoury dishes as can the larger, black cardamom. The latter is, however, rather bitter in taste and should be used sparingly.

Chilli (*mirch*) — as I have previously mentioned, small chillis are very hot and should be used with care. Chillis are the pods of a species of capsicum, and many varieties are available fresh, dried, or as chilli powder.

Cinnamon (*dalchini*) — this is the hard, dried inner bark of a tree, and is usually broken into pieces for use in curries, sweet dishes or in mulled wine.

Cloves (*laung*) — these are black with a distinctive medicinal smell and, although expensive, 1 oz (25g) will be enough for many dishes as they are used sparingly, whole or crushed, on account of their strong aroma.

Coconut (*naryal*) — I have already mentioned the disadvantage of fresh coconut being tedious in its preparation, and I strongly recommend the use of creamed coconut which can be bought in 7 oz (200g) slabs. It is easy to cut or grate and melts quickly when heated.

Coriander leaves/cilantro (*dhania*) — these can be bought in many continental food shops or grown in the garden. The plant quickly withers and turns yellow and so must be kept in the refrigerator or with its roots in water. The best way to preserve the leaves is to freeze them in small containers and then they can be used as required. To prepare the leaves, cut them from the stems using scissors and wash thoroughly. They can then be chopped and stirred into curries or used as a garnish.

Coriander seeds (dhania) — these are small, round and light brown. I suggest that you buy the seeds whole rather than ground and grind or pound them as required. They are used in most curries, batters and other savoury dishes.

Cumin (jeera) — this greyish-green seed has a pleasantly pungent aroma and can be used liberally in most savoury dishes, generally ground.

Fennel (sanf) — these small, pale green seeds have a distinctive flavour like aniseed and are used in certain curries.

Fenugreek (methi) — these small, hard seeds have a pleasant aromatic smell and may be used in most savoury dishes. They may also be sprouted and the sprouts used in salads.

Garam masala — this is a mixture of several ground spices such as cardamoms, cinnamon, cloves and cumin. It is usually added to the dish at a late stage in cooking, together with lemon or lime juice.

Ginger (adrak) — this is a root with a thin skin which should scrape off easily if the ginger is fresh. The flesh is somewhat woody, but it should be moist. It should be peeled and finely chopped. Although it is hot when eaten raw, when added to a curry it does not make it much hotter, and it is an aid to digestion. Do not substitute fresh ginger with ground or preserved ginger.

Gram flour (besan) — this is a fine flour, creamy yellow in colour, similar to soya flour, and is made from lentils. It is often used in batters, breads and to thicken certain curries. This is a whole grain flour and highly nutritious.

Mustard seed (rai) — the black mustard seed is used in Indian dishes. When fried whole they splutter, so care should be taken. They are used in curries, mainly wet ones such as tomato or *dhall*. They should not be over-used as they have a tendency to make a dish bitter though they do have a high nutritional value.

Paprika — this red powder is ground from dried red peppers, and usually originates from Hungary or Spain. It may be used liberally as it is not nearly as hot as chilli powder for which it may be substituted in many recipes.

Pistachio nuts — these are widely used in Indian sweet dishes, but they can be ground and used as an ingredient in a curry paste. Their high cost will prevent any wild experimentation.

Poppy seeds (*khus khus*) — these minute white seeds are occasionally used in curries mainly to thicken the sauce in which the curry is cooking. The black variety are used in certain cakes and breads from Eastern Europe.

Saffron (*kesar*) — these red or orange strands from the stamen of the saffron crocus are highly expensive, but they can be used in small quantities to colour and flavour rice and in desserts.

Tamarind (*imli*) — this is the seed pod of a tropical tree. It should be soaked in boiling water for at least one hour and the liquid strained off to give curries and some fresh chutneys a certain tartness. It is possible to substitute lemon or lime juice for tamarind water, but not vinegar.

Turmeric (*haldi*) — this comes in the form of a fine yellow powder which is a powerful dye, so keep it away from clothes, tablecloths and skin. It can be used sparingly in most curries. The powder is ground from a dried root similar to ginger, and it is worth while to make an effort to obtain fresh turmeric if you can.

SUGGESTED MENUS
for 6 people

Menu I	Menu II

Starters

Onion Bhajis	Mushroom Pakoras
Popadams	Popadams

Main Courses

Dhall	Tomato Curry
Chick Pea Curry	Peanut Curry
Vegetable Curry	Vegetable Curry
Cucumber Raita	Coconut Chutney
Mint and Coriander Chutney	Aubergine Bharta
Pilau Rice	Rotis

Desserts

Mango Fool	Srikand

RECIPES

A. Snacks — all deep-fried

ONION BHAJIS

Imperial (Metric)	American
½ lb (¼ kilo) gram flour	1½ cupsful gram flour
5 medium onions, shredded or coarsely grated	5 medium onions, shredded or coarsely grated
2 teaspoonsful cumin seeds, ground	2 teaspoonsful cumin seeds, ground
2 teaspoonsful coriander seeds, ground	2 teaspoonsful coriander seeds, ground
2 green chillis, finely chopped	2 green chillis, finely chopped
5 cloves garlic, crushed	5 cloves garlic, crushed
3 teaspoonsful sea salt	3 teaspoonsful sea salt
2 teaspoonsful fresh ginger, finely chopped	2 teaspoonsful fresh ginger, finely chopped
Water	Water
Vegetable oil for deep-frying	Vegetable oil for deep-frying

1. Mix all the ingredients together using enough water to make a thick batter which will hold together when dropped from a serving spoon.

2. Heat the oil until the batter rises to the surface as soon as it is dropped in. If the oil is not hot enough, the *bhajis* will be soggy.

3. Use a serving spoon to drop the batter into the oil. Up to 6 *bhajis* can be cooked simultaneously, depending on the size of the pan.

4. Using another spoon, preferably with holes in it, extract the cooked *bhajis* when they are brown. Also extract any smaller pieces of cooked batter which tend to fall away from the *bhajis*. Do not allow the oil to become too hot or the *bhajis* will not cook evenly.

5. Place the cooked *bhajis* on absorbent paper and serve while they are still hot.

Note: Onion *bhajis* dipped in cucumber *raita* are a delicious snack.

PAKORAS

For the batter:

Imperial (Metric)	American
6 oz (150g) gram flour	1 cupful gram flour
2 green chillis, finely chopped	2 green chillis, finely chopped
2 teaspoonsful cumin seeds, ground	2 teaspoonsful cumin seeds, ground
2 teaspoonsful coriander seeds, ground	2 teaspoonsful coriander seeds, ground
2 cloves garlic, crushed	2 cloves garlic, crushed
2 teaspoonsful sea salt	2 teaspoonsful sea salt
Water	Water

To dip in batter:

Imperial (Metric)	American
1 lb (1/2 kilo) button mushrooms	8 cupsful button mushrooms
2 large aubergines, cubed	2 large eggplants, cubed
Vegetable oil for deep-frying	Vegetable oil for deep-frying

1. Sift the gram flour into a bowl and mix with the other ingredients to form a thick batter to coat the vegetables.

2. Dip the mushrooms and aubergines (eggplants) into the batter and deep-fry in the oil, which must be sufficiently hot to make the *pakoras* rise to the surface of the oil as soon as they have been placed in it.

3. Cook the *pakoras* until the batter turns golden. Up to 10 *pakoras* may be cooked simultaneously, depending on the size of the pan. They should be placed into the pan singly so that they do not stick together.

4. Take the cooked *pakoras* from the oil with a clean spoon and place them on absorbent paper. Serve while they are still hot.

Note: Other vegetables which may be prepared in this way include courgettes (zucchini), cauliflower, cubed root vegetables, potato rounds (parboil these first), bamboo shoots, bananas, sliced onions and spinach.

POPADAMS

These are thin wafers made from lentil flour which can be bought ready-made in many shops. Plain popadams are nowhere near as good as the thinner and more tasty flavoured ones — usually garlic, red chilli or black pepper flavour.

Popadams
Vegetable oil

1. Pour just enough oil into a frying pan (skillet) to cover a *popadam* — about ½ in. (1cm) deep — and heat.

2. When placed into the oil, the *popadam* will go limp before it starts to fry. At this moment it is possible to fold the *popadam* in half, using two spatulas, one to hold the *popadam* down and the other to fold it over.

3. To ensure flatness of the *popadam*, continually press down the surface with the spatulas, moving them from place to place on the surface of the *popadam*.

4. After 5 seconds turn the folded *popadam*.

5. After a further 5 seconds both sides should be crisp and golden. Remove the *popadam* from the pan.

6. Place the *popadams* in a toast-rack or arrange them in a dish so that any surplus oil can drain off. If you have room in your oven, place the *popadams* in it so that they will keep hot and become completely dry.

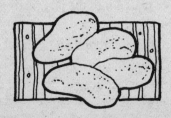

B. Curries

PEANUT CURRY

Imperial (Metric)	American
2 tablespoonsful vegetable oil	2 tablespoonsful vegetable oil
4 medium onions, finely chopped	4 medium onions, finely chopped
1 teaspoonful cumin seeds, ground	1 teaspoonful cumin seeds, ground
1 teaspoonful coriander seeds, ground	1 teaspoonful coriander seeds, ground
1 teaspoonful poppy seeds	1 teaspoonful poppy seeds
½ teaspoonful turmeric	½ teaspoonful turmeric
3 green chillis, finely chopped	3 green chillis, finely chopped
1 lb (½ kilo) raw peanuts	3 cupsful raw peanuts
14 oz (400g) tin tomatoes	1 medium can tomatoes
2 teaspoonsful Demerara sugar	2 teaspoonsful Demerara sugar
2 teaspoonsful sea salt	2 teaspoonsful sea salt
½ pint (¼ litre) water	1⅓ cupsful water

1. Heat the oil and fry the onions until transparent.

2. Add the spices and continue to fry for 5 minutes.

3. Stir in the nuts, tomatoes, sugar and salt. Fry for 2 minutes.

4. Add the water, stir well and simmer until the nuts are tender — this will take over an hour. Add more water if necessary.

5. Serve garnished with chopped coriander leaves (cilantro).

Note: Grated fresh coconut goes well with this curry.

DHALL

Imperial (Metric)	American
1 lb (½ kilo) lentils	2 cupsful lentils
1 teaspoonful sea salt	1 teaspoonful sea salt
4 tablespoonsful vegetable oil	4 tablespoonsful vegetable oil
2 teaspoonsful mustard seeds	2 teaspoonsful mustard seeds
4 medium onions, finely chopped	4 medium onions, finely chopped
8 cloves garlic, crushed	8 cloves garlic, crushed
4 green cardamoms, pounded	4 green cardamoms, pounded
2 pieces cinnamon, broken into small pieces	2 pieces cinnamon, broken into small pieces
4 cloves, crushed	4 cloves, crushed
3 teaspoonsful coriander seeds, ground	3 teaspoonsful coriander seeds, ground
2 teaspoonsful turmeric	2 teaspoonsful turmeric
2 teaspoonsful paprika	2 teaspoonsful paprika
2 teaspoonsful cumin seeds, ground	2 teaspoonsful cumin seeds, ground

1. Wash the lentils, removing any small stones and husks, and soak for a few hours. (Soaking is not essential if you use *toor dhall* or if you are using a pressure cooker.)

2. Drain the lentils and bring them to the boil with salt in enough water to cover them. You will need to add more water as the lentils are cooking, but avoid using too much water as the final dish should not be at all runny.

3. Cook the lentils on a medium heat until they are soft. If you have a liquidizer, this may be used to make a smoother *dhall*.

4. Heat the oil and fry the mustard seeds until they pop.

5. Add the onions and continue to fry for 3 minutes before adding the garlic and other spices.

6. Stir in the lentils and mix well.

7. Simmer until the dish is of the right consistency.

Note: This dish may be varied by adding coconut or yogurt to the *dhall*. Spinach and celery can also be incorporated to good effect, or tomato *purée* can be used to give a taste and colour variation.

TOMATO CURRY

Imperial (Metric)	American
3 x 14 oz (400g) tins tomatoes	3 medium cans tomatoes
1 teaspoonful raw cane sugar	1 teaspoonful raw cane sugar
2 teaspoonsful sea salt	2 teaspoonsful sea salt
2 oz (50g) gram flour	5 tablespoonsful gram flour
4 tablespoonsful tamarind water (or use lemon juice)	4 tablespoonsful tamarind water (or use lemon juice)
½ pint (¼ litre) water	1⅓ cupsful water
2 tablespoonsful vegetable oil	2 tablespoonsful vegetable oil
½ teaspoonful fennel seeds	½ teaspoonful fennel seeds
1 teaspoonful cumin seeds	1 teaspoonful cumin seeds
1 teaspoonful mustard seeds	1 teaspoonful mustard seeds
½ teaspoonful fenugreek seeds	½ teaspoonful fenugreek seeds
2 green chillis, finely chopped (discard the pips)	2 green chillis, finely chopped (discard the pips)
½ teaspoonful turmeric	½ teaspoonful turmeric
3 tablespoonsful coriander leaves, chopped	3 tablespoonsful cilantro, chopped

1. Place the tomatoes, sugar and salt into a saucepan and bring them to the boil.

2. Cook the tomatoes on a medium heat, stirring occasionally, for 30 minutes. Allow to cool.

3. *Purée* the tomatoes in a blender or whisk until smooth.

4. Sift the flour into a bowl and add the tamarind water, mixing well until you have a smooth, thick paste.

5. Add the water, stirring constantly.

6. Pour in the tomato mixture and mix well.

7. In another pan, heat the oil and add the fennel, cumin, mustard and fenugreek seeds.

8. After three minutes throw in the chillis and add the turmeric.

9. Add the liquid sauce gradually and bring to the boil, then cover, lower the heat and simmer for one hour, stirring occasionally.

10. Add more salt or water if necessary, and finally the coriander leaves.

CHICK PEA CURRY
Chick peas are also called garbanzos or channa dahl, and are a very rich source of protein.

Imperial (Metric)	American
1 lb (½ kilo) chick peas	2 cupsful garbanzo beans
4 cloves	4 cloves
1 piece cinnamon, broken	1 piece cinnamon, broken
4 green cardamoms, pounded	4 green cardamoms, pounded
2 green chillis, or dried red chillis	2 green chillis, or dried red chillis
1 in. (2½cm) piece ginger, chopped small	1 in. (2½cm) piece ginger, chopped small
3 tablespoonsful vegetable oil	3 tablespoonsful vegetable oil
4 medium onions, finely chopped	4 medium onions, finely chopped
4 cloves garlic, crushed	4 cloves garlic, crushed
1 teaspoonful paprika	1 teaspoonful paprika
2 teaspoonsful turmeric	2 teaspoonsful turmeric
1 teaspoonful cumin seeds, ground	1 teaspoonful cumin seeds, ground
1 teaspoonful coriander seeds, ground	1 teaspoonful coriander seeds, ground
Coriander leaves	Cilantro leaves
Tamarind water	Tamarind water

1. Soak the chick peas (garbanzo beans) overnight in a generous amount of water. They will swell up considerably.

2. Bring the chick peas (garbanzo beans) to the boil in fresh water.

Add the cloves, cinnamon, cardamoms, chillis and ginger.

3. Simmer until the chick peas (garbanzo beans) are tender, adding more water if necessary.

4. When they are cooked, remove the chick peas (garbanzo beans) from the heat and drain them in a colander. Extract as many of the whole spices as you can from the chick peas (garbanzo beans).

5. Heat the vegetable oil and fry the onion and garlic until transparent.

6. Add the other spices and fry for a further 5 minutes, stirring frequently.

7. Add the chick peas (garbanzo beans) and stir gently until they are well mixed with the spice mixture.

8. Mix in the coriander leaves (cilantro) and tamarind water with some of the drained stock. This dish can be kept warm in an oven while the cooker top is used for the other curries.

Note: Yogurt may be added to this dish in place of tamarind water.

VEGETABLE CURRY

Imperial (Metric)	American
2 lb (1 kilo) vegetables	2 pounds vegetables
4 tablespoonsful vegetable oil	4 tablespoonsful vegetable oil
4 medium onions, finely chopped	4 medium onions, finely chopped
3 cloves garlic, crushed	3 cloves garlic, crushed
1 in. (2½cm) piece ginger, finely chopped	1 in. (2½cm) piece ginger, finely chopped
2 teaspoonsful cumin seeds, ground	2 teaspoonsful cumin seeds, ground
2 teaspoonsful coriander seeds, ground	2 teaspoonsful coriander seeds, ground
1 teaspoonful turmeric	1 teaspoonful turmeric
1 teaspoonful fenugreek, ground	1 teaspoonful fenugreek, ground
½ teaspoonful mustard seeds, ground	½ teaspoonful mustard seeds, ground
1 teaspoonful paprika	1 teaspoonful paprika
14 oz (400g) tin tomatoes	1 medium can tomatoes

1. Parboil root vegetables such as carrots and potatoes for 10 minutes. It is better to dice the vegetables before parboiling.

2. Heat the vegetable oil and fry the onions with the garlic and ginger for 5 or so minutes.

3. Add the spices and continue to fry for a further 5 minutes.

4. Add the tin of tomatoes or use 3 tablespoonsful of tomato *purée*.

5. Add the vegetables: first the *bhindis*, green beans or aubergines (eggplants), followed by leeks, cauliflower, courgettes (zucchini), the parboiled root vegetables and, finally, the mushrooms. About 5 different vegetables should be used, depending on their availability and your own personal preferences.

6. Add a little stock from the parboiled vegetables.

7. Cook gently for an hour or so until the vegetables are tender, stirring occasionally to prevent sticking. Do not allow the

vegetables to become mushy.

8.   Decorate with grated fresh coconut or coriander leaves (cilantro).

C. Curry Accompaniments

CUCUMBER RAITA

Imperial (Metric)	American
1 large cucumber	1 large cucumber
1 pint (½ litre) yogurt	2½ cupsful yogurt
Pinch paprika	Pinch paprika

1.   Grate the unpeeled cucumber and squeeze out the juice. Alternatively, the cucumber may be cut into matchstick size pieces.

2.   Mix the yogurt with the cucumber.

3.   Sprinkle paprika carefully on top.

Note: This *raita* may be varied by including fresh chillis, coconut, sultanas (golden seedless raisins), pistachio nuts, mint, shredded onion or coriander leaves (cilantro). Sliced banana also makes an excellent *raita*.

MINT AND CORIANDER CHUTNEY

Imperial (Metric)
4 tablespoonsful lemon juice
1 teaspoonful raw cane sugar
4 tablespoonsful fresh mint, finely
  chopped
6 tablespoonsful fresh coriander,
  finely chopped
2 red chillis, finely chopped (optional)
1/2 teaspoonful sea salt

American
4 tablespoonsful lemon juice
1 teaspoonful raw cane sugar
4 tablespoonsful fresh mint, finely
  chopped
1/2 cupful cilantro, finely chopped
2 red chillis, finely chopped (optional)
1/2 teaspoonful sea salt

1. Sweeten the lemon juice with the sugar.

2. Add the other ingredients and mix well.

Note: A spicier flavour can be imparted using a teaspoonful of ground cumin seeds and the chutney may be made more substantial by the addition of 2 tablespoonsful of ground roasted peanuts.

AUBERGINE BHARTA

Imperial (Metric)
2 lb (1 kilo) aubergines
1 medium onion, finely chopped
2 tablespoonsful vegetable oil
14 oz (400g) tin tomatoes
1 teaspoonful coriander seeds,
  ground
1 teaspoonful cumin seeds, ground
1/2 teaspoonful turmeric
1 green chilli (discard the seeds)
1 tablespoonful coriander leaves,
  chopped
1 1/2 teaspoonsful sea salt

American
2 pounds eggplants
1 medium onion, finely chopped
2 tablespoonsful vegetable oil
1 medium can tomatoes
1 teaspoonful coriander seeds,
  ground
1 teaspoonful cumin seeds, ground
1/2 teaspoonful turmeric
1 green chilli (discard the seeds)
1 tablespoonful cilantro, chopped
1 1/2 teaspoonsful sea salt

1. If you have a rotisserie, roast the aubergines (eggplants) on it until their skins darken and they are soft. Otherwise, roast the

aubergines (eggplants) in a hot oven (stove).

2. Allow the aubergines (eggplants) to cool before peeling them. Place the peeled aubergines (eggplants) in a blender and blend until smooth. If you do not have an electric blender, the aubergines (eggplants) can be mashed.

3. Fry the onion until transparent in the oil.

4. Add the tomatoes, having drained off the juice.

5. Add the spices and continue to fry for a further 5 minutes.

6. Add the aubergine (eggplant) *purée*, coriander leaves (cilantro) and sea salt and mix well.

7. Allow to cool before serving as a side dish.

COCONUT CHUTNEY

Imperial (Metric)	American
½ fresh coconut	½ fresh coconut
1 tablespoonful fresh ginger, grated	1 tablespoonful fresh ginger, grated
1 tablespoonful lemon juice	1 tablespoonful lemon juice
1 pint (½ litre) plain yogurt	2½ cupsful plain yogurt
A few green chillis, finely chopped (optional)	A few green chillis, finely chopped (optional)
2 tablespoonsful coriander leaves, finely chopped	2 tablespoonsful cilantro, finely chopped

1. Grate the coconut flesh. If you have a food processor, this job will be much simplified.

2. Mix well with the other ingredients and garnish with coriander leaves.

Note: A few raisins would make an interesting addition to this chutney.

D. Rice and Rotis

PILAU RICE

Imperial (Metric)	American
2 tablespoonsful vegetable oil	2 tablespoonsful vegetable oil
½ teaspoonful turmeric	½ teaspoonful turmeric
2 bay leaves	2 bay leaves
2 cardamoms	2 cardamoms
2 pieces cinnamon	2 pieces cinnamon
4 cloves	4 cloves
1 lb (½ kilo) long grain brown rice	2½ cupsful long grain brown rice
1 teaspoonful sea salt	1 teaspoonful sea salt

1. Heat the oil and add the turmeric followed by the other spices.

2. Add the rice and stir over a medium heat for a minute or so.

3. Pour in sufficient water to cover the rice and 1 in. (2½cm) depth of water extra.

4. Add the salt and bring to the boil.

5. Turn down the heat and simmer, covered, for 45 minutes.

6. Let the rice stand for a further 10 minutes, still covered, before removing the lid and serving.

Note: It is a good idea to add a few blanched almonds or cooked peas before serving. Two quartered hard-boiled eggs or some thinly sliced fried onion can be used as a garnish.

ROTIS

Imperial (Metric)	American
1 lb (½ kilo) wholemeal flour	4 cupsful wholewheat flour
Good pinch of sea salt	Good pinch of sea salt
½ pint (300ml) of water	1⅓ cupsful of water
4 oz (100g) vegetable fat	½ cupful vegetable fat

1. Mix the flour with the sea salt.

2. Add enough water to make a soft dough and knead well for 15 minutes.

3. Leave to stand for 30 minutes.

4. Divide into small round balls (12 to 15) and roll out, brushing each several times with the melted vegetable fat before folding and rolling out again.

5. Place each roti between sheets of greaseproof paper until you have finished the rolling process and then fry the rotis in vegetable fat until brown but not crisp.

Note: The rotis should be puffy so each may be stuffed with a spicy mashed potato filling and served as a snack with chutney or *raita*.

E. Desserts

MANGO FOOL

Imperial (Metric)	American
4 oz (100g) creamed coconut	4 ounces creamed coconut
8 white cardamoms	8 white cardamoms
1 large tin mango *purée*	1 large tin mango *purée*
1 tablespoonful lemon juice	1 tablespoonful lemon juice
½ pint (¼ litre) double cream, whisked	1⅓ cupsful heavy cream, whisked

1. Put a little water in a saucepan and, over a gentle heat, melt the creamed coconut.

2. Remove the black seeds from the centre of the cardamoms and discard the husks. Crush the seeds or grind them in a spice grinder.

3. Combine the mango *purée*, coconut, lemon juice and cardamoms.

4. Spoon into wineglasses and allow to stand in the refrigerator for an hour or so.

5. Pipe cream round the edge of each glass or stir it into the mango to create a whirl of white in the orange colouring.

SRIKAND

The effort and forethought required to make this creamy dessert is worth while because of its unique character.

Imperial (Metric)	American
2 pints (1 litre) plain yogurt	5 cupsful plain yogurt
8 white cardamoms	8 white cardamoms
A pinch of saffron	A pinch of saffron
1 tablespoonful rosewater	1 tablespoonful rosewater
4 oz (100g) raw cane sugar	3/4 cupful raw cane sugar
2 tablespoonsful cashews, coarsely chopped	2 tablespoonsful cashews, coarsely chopped
2 tablespoonsful raisins, coarsely chopped	2 tablespoonsful raisins, coarsely chopped

1. Put the yogurt in a muslin bag and allow to drain overnight. The solid residue is similar to curd cheese and curd cheese could be used instead of the yogurt if you do not wish to make it yourself.

2. Remove the black seeds from the centre of the cardamoms and discard the husks. Crush the seeds or grind them in your spice grinder.

3. Dissolve the saffron in the rosewater.

4. Combine all the ingredients and mix well.

5. Place in a refrigerator to chill.

6. Serve garnished possibly with a maraschino cherry or a few chopped pistachios.

2.

ITALY

Many different and distinctive flavours combine to give Italian food its worldwide appeal. Although the dishes made in the different regions of Italy vary with local tastes, traditions, climate and terrain, they are characterized by certain ingredients such as pasta, herbs, cheese and tomatoes. It is also true that the best Italian food is to be tasted in the home, and not in hotels or restaurants, so the target of creating dishes more exotic than your guests will ever have tasted can easily be achieved.

The main herbs used in Italian cookery are my favourites — basil and oregano — and I make generous use of them in the dishes which make up this chapter. There are over fifty varieties of basil that grow in Italy, but it is a small-leaved variety which grows around Genoa that is the inspiration for pesto, a superbly aromatic pâté which is often used as a sauce for pasta. Parsley is another important herb in Italian cookery, and one you are more likely to be able to obtain fresh. Fortunately, dried basil and oregano are easily available from wholefood suppliers.

Tomatoes and tomato *purée* are used liberally in Italian recipes. It is more economical to buy tomato *purée* in large tins and freeze any that you have not used in ice cube containers. Tinned tomatoes are usually of Italian origin and so are most suitable for the recipes in this chapter, besides which they are very economical. Fresh, firm tomatoes are needed for slicing for Tomatoes with Pesto. This makes a perfect starter for the meal because it combines so many of the flavours predominant in Italian food, and yet it is unlikely to impair any guest's appetite.

It has been said that Italian food is all oil and garlic, and while it is true that garlic features in most Italian recipes, including the ones in this chapter, it is always used by the Italians with discretion. The lasagne and vegetable dishes of this dinner party would lack a certain zest or aromatic quality if garlic were omitted altogether, yet the quantity should be varied according to personal taste, and the variation in the size of garlic cloves means that the number suggested in any recipe is only a guide.

In many parts of Italy, olive oil is the main cooking fat, and I use a large quantity of it for frying, in sauces and in pâtés. The lighter coloured refined olive oil lacks the flavour of the thicker, pale-green oil which you should do your best to obtain. I would also advise you to buy olive oil in large tins (about four litres in capacity) as it is more economical and can easily be decanted into large glass bottles where it will keep indefinitely. Also, it is wise to ensure that it is a virgin oil, which means that it is from the first pressing, and it should be cold-pressed. The olives themselves are used in several recipes in this chapter. Both green and black olives are available in different sizes in all good Greek and Italian delicatessens. The riper black olives can easily be stoned by halving them, and the smaller and firmer olives are best pitted by cutting away the flesh in a spiral so that it can be re-formed to make a whole olive. For the lazy, pitted olives can be purchased, and a kitchen tool is available that will pit smaller olives as well as cherries.

Lemons, lemon juice and wine vinegar are further common ingredients in Italian sauces. A lemon with a fresh appearance should be chosen for the Tomato and Red Wine Sauce as the pared rind is an important part of the aromatic quality of the sauce.

If the above mentioned ingredients combine to give the distinctive flavours, it is the pasta and cheeses which form the bulk of the Italian vegetarian dinner party. There are many shapes of pasta and it may be bought dried, or, if you are lucky, fresh. In fact, if you ask for fresh pasta in a good Italian delicatessen, it will soon be produced for you, even if it is not on display. Wholewheat spaghetti, macaroni and lasagne are available in shops dealing in wholefoods, and increasingly from supermarkets.

It would be wrong not to mention here another great Italian vegetarian dish, risotto, which is not included in this dinner party. Risotto involves cooking the rice in a special way, adding stock from time to time as the rice is cooking on a low heat. This method of cooking is quite different from that of making pilau rice, and it necessitates constant stirring to avoid sticking.

The cheeses which I have used in this dinner party include Ricotta, Parmesan, Pecorino Sardo and Mozzarella. Ricotta is a soft, white cheese which can be used in making cheesecake as well as in many savoury dishes including the lasagne dish of this chapter. If Ricotta cannot be obtained, curd cheese is an acceptable substitute. Parmesan is a peer among cheeses. It is aged for at least two years, often for four, and while its claim to fame is as a cooking cheese without equal, it is an excellent table cheese when eaten freshly cut. Even when it is used for cooking in its grated form, it should be freshly grated from a piece rather then bought ready grated. Pecorino can be used instead of Parmesan in many recipes as it is an excellent table cheese, slightly smoother than Parmesan. It is made from ewe's milk while Mozzarella is made from buffalo's milk in many parts of southern Italy. Mozzarella made with cow's milk originating from such unlikely places as Scotland and Denmark, is available in most supermarkets and delicatessens. It has a soft, spongy texture and is not easy to slice or grate. Most of the ingredients mentioned above are available in most good continental delicatessens.

Since cheese and fruit bring an Italian meal to a natural close, and since there are so many fine cheeses available that should be part of an Italian dinner party, I have no hesitation in suggesting cheese and fruit as an ideal final course. Among the cheeses that could make up your Italian cheese board are Dolcelatte, Gorgonzola, Parmesan, Taleggio and Fontina. Peaches, apples, pears, oranges, and grapes could make up a most refreshing fruit bowl to accompany the cheese, along with the more traditional crispbreads and rolls. Alternatively, peaches in white wine are a most delicious and refreshing ending to an Italian meal and can be prepared quickly and well in advance of the meal.

Italian wine is as legendary as Italian food, and it is often used as

an ingredient in regional dishes. Chianti is an excellent choice as a
red wine to accompany this dinner party, while Soave is a reliable
white wine. Valpolicella and Bardolino are table wines suitable for
use in the recipes requiring wine, or for drinking. The sparkling wine,
Spumante, would be my choice as an accompaniment to the starter
of Tomatoes with Pesto.

SUGGESTED MENUS
for 6 people

Menu I   **Menu II**

Starters

Tomatoes with Pesto   Polenta and Pesto

Main Courses

Lasagne al Forno   Pizza
Aubergine Salad   Peppers in Olive Oil
Peppers in Olive Oil   Simple Green Salad
(lettuce, cucumber,
pepper, watercress)

Desserts

Cheeseboard   Peaches in White Wine
Fresh Fruit

RECIPES

A. Starters

TOMATOES WITH PESTO

This is a superb starter as it can easily be handed round while your guests are enjoying their pre-dinner drinks. It includes many of the chief flavours in Italian cooking and will put your guests in the right mood for the meal to come, as the aroma and taste of pesto will stimulate even the dullest of appetites.

Imperial (Metric)	American
2 tablespoonsful basil (use fresh if available)	2 tablespoonsful basil (use fresh if available)
3 tablespoonsful olive oil	3 tablespoonsful olive oil
½ teaspoonful sea salt	½ teaspoonful sea salt
1 oz (25g) Pecorino Sardo, finely grated	¼ cupful Pecorino Sardo, finely grated
1 oz (25g) Parmesan, finely grated	¼ cupful Parmesan, finely grated
2 cloves garlic, crushed	2 cloves garlic, crushed
1½ lb (¾ kilo) large, firm tomatoes	1½ pounds large, firm tomatoes
Parsley	Parsley

1. Mix the basil and olive oil well with the sea salt.

2. Add the cheeses and garlic.

3. Cut each tomato into 3-4 slices.

4. Place a heaped teaspoonful of pesto on each tomato slice.

5. Carefully arrange a leaf of parsley on each slice, and put the dish in a cool place until it is required.

POLENTA

Polenta is a fine maize flour, which is very cheap and yet capable of being made into a tasty part of this meal to complement the strong flavours of the other dishes. Polenta is a common staple food in much of northern Italy and it can be eaten just with a topping of thick mushroom or tomato sauce and cheese. In Italy it is ladled onto a large round wooden board and cut with a wire in the same way as cheese is often cut. I prefer to let the Polenta set in a baking tray at least 2 in. (5cm) deep, and cut it out with a palette knife before it is fried.

Imperial (Metric)	American
1 ¾ pints (1 litre) water	4 cupsful water
½ lb (¼ kilo) polenta	2 cupsful polenta
Sea salt	Sea salt
2 oz (50g) polyunsaturated margarine	4 tablespoonsful polyunsaturated margarine
2 oz (50g) Parmesan, grated	½ cupful Parmesan, grated
1 egg, beaten	1 egg, beaten
Dry fine breadcrumbs	Dry fine breadcrumbs
Olive oil for frying	Olive oil for frying

1. Bring the water to the boil in a large saucepan.

2. Pour in the polenta slowly, stirring constantly to avoid lumps. Use a long wooden spoon to stir the polenta as it has a tendency to 'spit' while it is being cooked.

3. Add the salt and margarine.

4. Cook on a low heat for 20 minutes until it is thick but smooth and soft. When it is ready it should come away from the sides of the pan as you stir.

5. Add the Parmesan cheese.

6. Pour the polenta into a greased tin which is at least 2 in. (5cm) deep.

7. Allow the polenta to cool and set — an hour should be sufficient.

8. When the polenta is solid, cut it into small squares, or use a rinsed inverted glass to make rounds.

9. Dip each piece into beaten egg and roll in breadcrumbs.

10. Fry in olive oil until golden brown all over. Drain on kitchen paper.

Note: If you are serving Polenta as a starter, you could top with a sauce and cheese, preferably Mozzarella, or serve with a sauce such as Pesto (page 43).

B. Main Courses

TOMATO AND RED WINE SAUCE

The superb aroma of this sauce will drive members of your household crazy with hunger when they smell it cooking. Do not be deterred by its early thinness as it thickens well in the course of cooking.

Imperial (Metric)	American
6 tablespoonsful olive oil	6 tablespoonsful olive oil
4 medium onions, finely chopped	4 medium onions, finely chopped
4 cloves garlic, crushed	4 cloves garlic, crushed
½ lb (¼ kilo) mushrooms, sliced	4 cupsful mushrooms, sliced
1 tablespoonful dried basil	1 tablespoonful dried basil
2 tablespoonsful dried oregano	2 tablespoonsful dried oregano
2 tablespoonsful parsley, finely chopped	2 tablespoonsful parsley, finely chopped
¾ lb (350g) tomato *purée*	1½ cupsful tomato paste
Peel of 1 lemon	Peel of 1 lemon
4 bay leaves	4 bay leaves
Sea salt	Sea salt
Black pepper, freshly ground	Black pepper, freshly ground
1 bottle red wine	1 bottle red wine
¾ pint (400ml) vegetable stock	2 cupsful vegetable stock

1. Heat the oil and fry the onions and garlic until they become transparent.

2. Add the sliced mushrooms, basil, oregano and chopped parsley. Stir and fry for a minute or so.

3. Add the tomato *purée*, lemon peel, bay leaves, sea salt and black pepper.

4. Lastly, add the wine and some of the stock. Add the remainder of the stock later if it is required — the sauce should be thick but easy to pour.

5. Let the sauce simmer for an hour or so until it is required in the

following recipe. The sauce may be made well in advance and kept in a jar in the refrigerator.

PEPPERS IN OLIVE OIL

The peppers should be roasted in a very hot oven until their skins blacken. Only then will it be possible to peel the skin from the peppers, but care must be taken as their juices will be very hot and should be drained off before any attempt is made to peel them. All the effort involved is well worth while because the sweet fresh taste of this side dish is an ideal complement to the richness of the lasagne and the pizza.

Imperial (Metric)	American
2 lb (1 kilo) peppers, red and green	2 pounds peppers, red and green
4 oz (100g) black olives, stoned	4 ounces black olives, stoned
3 cloves garlic, crushed	3 cloves garlic, crushed
Sea salt	Sea salt
4 tablespoonsful olive oil	4 tablespoonsful olive oil
1 tablespoonful lemon juice	1 tablespoonful lemon juice
Parsley, finely chopped	Parsley, finely chopped

1. Roast the peppers in a very hot oven until their skins are blackened.

2. Let them cool slightly, pierce them with a knife to allow the natural moisture to escape, remove the skins and discard the seeds and pith.

3. Cut the peppers into matchstick-size strips.

4. Arrange the strips in a bowl and combine them with the olives.

5. Mix in the garlic and a little salt.

6. Pour the olive oil and lemon juice over the peppers and decorate with parsley. Serve cold.

LASAGNE AL FORNO

Many variations upon the basic theme of pasta in layers with sauces, cheeses and vegetables are possible. The one important rule is that no pasta should be visible when the dish is put into the oven, as it will quickly dry up and become tough.

Some variations of this dish use Bolognese Sauce and a vegetarian version can easily be concocted. It is also possible to use a béchamel sauce instead of, or together with, the other sauces mentioned, and vegetables that can be used as layers are aubergines (eggplants) and courgettes (zucchini).

You may prefer to use a wide dish with fewer layers of lasagne, or a deeper dish with more layers. The latter allows for more flexibility as a smaller quantity of each layer is needed. Avoid filling the dish to the brim as a certain amount of expansion takes place.

Here is my favourite version of the dish. Exact quantities are not important but I find that the amount of lasagne mentioned is quite sufficient, whereas there is rarely too much sauce.

Imperial (Metric)	American
2 medium onions, finely chopped	2 medium onions, finely chopped
2 cloves garlic, crushed	2 cloves garlic, crushed
2 tablespoonsful olive oil	2 tablespoonsful olive oil
3 eggs, beaten	3 eggs, beaten
1½ lb (¾ kilo) Ricotta cheese	3 cupsful Ricotta cheese
6 oz (150g) Parmesan, grated	1½ cupsful Parmesan, grated
2 lb (1 kilo) spinach, cooked and finely chopped (frozen spinach is convenient)	2 pounds spinach, cooked and finely chopped (frozen spinach is convenient)
Sea salt	Sea salt
Black pepper, freshly ground	Black pepper, freshly ground
4 tablespoonsful parsley, finely chopped	4 tablespoonsful parsley, finely chopped
½ lb (¼ kilo) Mozzarella cheese	8 ounces Mozzarella cheese
1 lb (½ kilo) wholemeal lasagne	1 pound wholewheat lasagne
Tomato and Red Wine Sauce (page 46)	Tomato and Red Wine Sauce (page 46)

1. *For the Ricotta mix:* fry the onions and garlic in the olive oil until they become transparent.

2. Add the eggs to the Ricotta and mix well.

3. Mix in the Parmesan, fried onion and garlic, and the spinach (squeeze surplus liquid from the spinach and use as stock).

4. Add the sea salt, freshly ground black pepper and chopped fresh parsley.

5. *For the Mozzarella:* grate or slice the Mozzarella as thinly as possible.

6. *For the Lasagne:* half fill a large pan with salted water and add a tablespoonful of olive oil. Bring the water to the boil and drop three or four sheets of lasagne into the pan carefully. It should be cooked in about 12 minutes (or 4 minutes if it is freshly made lasagne). It should rise to the surface and be *al dente* (barely tender) when ready.

7. Lay the cooked lasagne separately on a damp, clean, white cloth to drain.

8. *For the assembly:* grease a large oven-proof dish, or use two or three smaller ones.

9. Arrange the ingredients in layers: lasagne, Ricotta mix, Mozzarella, and Tomato and Red Wine Sauce.

10. Cover the dish with a lid or with foil and bake at 350°F/180°C (Gas Mark 4) for 40 minutes.

11. Remove the lid and cook for a further 20 minutes, possibly with a little grated Parmesan scattered over.

PIZZA

Various traditional pizza recipes exist but many of their ingredients are the same as those used in the lasagne dish. This pizza recipe contrasts with these rather rich ingredients and makes an ideal main course whatever the occasion.

For the base:

Imperial (Metric)	American
3 teaspoonsful baking powder	3 teaspoonsful baking soda
¾ lb (350g) wholemeal flour	3 cupsful wholewheat flour
4 oz (100g) polyunsaturated margarine	½ cupful polyunsaturated margarine
6 oz (150g) Cheddar cheese, grated	1½ cupsful Cheddar cheese, grated
1 medium onion, grated	1 medium onion, grated
2 eggs	2 eggs

For the filling:

Imperial (Metric)	American
4 medium onions, finely chopped	4 medium onions, finely chopped
4 sticks celery, finely chopped	4 stalks celery, finely chopped
4 tablespoonsful olive oil	4 tablespoonsful olive oil
½ lb (¼ kilo) mushrooms, sliced	4 cupsful mushrooms, sliced
2 × 14 oz (400g) tins tomatoes	2 medium cans tomatoes
Sea salt	Sea salt
Freshly ground black pepper	Freshly ground black pepper
2 tablespoonsful basil	2 tablespoonsful basil
1 tablespoonful thyme	1 tablespoonful thyme
3 cloves garlic, crushed	3 cloves garlic, crushed
1 lb (½ kilo) Cheddar cheese, grated	5½ cupsful Cheddar cheese, grated
Black olives	Black olives

1. *For the base:* Mix the baking powder (baking soda) with the flour.

2. Rub in the margarine.

3. Add the cheese and grated onion.

4. Add the eggs and mix really well until the pastry is soft. Cover and put aside while you make the filling.

5. *For the filling:* put the onions and celery in a pan with the oil and fry for 5 minutes.

6. Add the sliced mushrooms and cook for a further 5 minutes.

7. Add the tomatoes, seasoning, garlic and herbs and mix in well.

8. Remove the filling from the heat and put it into a sieve or colander for a short while to allow excess liquid to run off.

9. Mix half of the cheese into the filling.

10. Roll out the dough and press into 2 large flan tins or use 1 large rectangular tray.

11. Fill the pies and garnish with olives and the remaining cheese.

12. Bake in a hot oven at 450°F/230°C (Gas Mark 8) for 15 to 20 minutes.

AUBERGINE SALAD

This salad may be served hot or cold and it can be varied, but its piquancy is an important contrast to the other flavours in the meal.

Imperial (Metric)	American
2 large aubergines, cubed	2 large eggplants, cubed
Sea salt and pepper	Sea salt and pepper
Olive oil for frying	Olive oil for frying
6 sticks celery, chopped	6 stalks celery, chopped
14 oz (400g) tin tomatoes	1 medium can tomatoes
⅓ pint (200ml) red wine vinegar	¾ cupful red wine vinegar
2 tablespoonsful sultanas	2 tablespoonsful golden seedless
4 oz (100g) green olives, stoned	raisins
3 tablespoonsful capers	4 ounces green olives, stoned
1 tablespoonful honey	3 tablespoonsful capers
3 lemon wedges	1 tablespoonful honey
	3 lemon wedges

1. Cube the aubergines (eggplants) and sprinkle with sea salt. Leave in a bowl with a heavy plate on top for an hour or so.

2. Wash and drain the aubergines (eggplants) and fry the cubes, a few at a time, in the olive oil until they are tender.

3. Fry the celery then add the tomatoes and the remaining ingredients including the aubergines (eggplants).

4. Cook gently for 10 minutes. Serve hot or cold as required, garnished with lemon wedges.

C. Dessert

PEACHES IN WHITE WINE

Imperial (Metric)	American
6 peaches	6 peaches
2 tablespoonsful raw cane sugar	2 tablespoonsful raw cane sugar
4 tablespoonsful water	4 tablespoonsful water
¼ bottle (175ml) sweet white wine	¼ bottle sweet white wine
1 tablespoonful Kirsch	1 tablespoonful Kirsch
½ pint (¼ litre) double cream, whipped	1⅓ cupsful heavy cream, whipped
6 Maraschino cherries	6 Maraschino cherries

1. Put the peaches in boiling water for 30 seconds. You should then be able to peel them quite easily.

2. Warm the water and dissolve the raw cane sugar in it.

3. Halve and stone the peaches and place in a bowl.

4. Pour the syrup, wine and Kirsch over the peaches and allow to stand in a cool place for several hours.

5. Place two halves in each dessert dish with some juice and pipe cream over them attractively.

6. Top with a Maraschino cherry just before serving.

3.

THE WEST INDIES

The colourful way of life of the folk who live in this area is reflected in their food. Even more important are the diverse origins of the dishes in different islands. This is because of the visits and colonization of islands by people from many countries and areas of the world who have made their own adaptation of recipes of their native countries using local ingredients. Since the time of colonization by Europeans, Africans, Indians and settlers from other parts of the Far East, specialities from one island have become established dishes elsewhere and so it is not always possible to name a specific place of origin of a dish. Nevertheless, there are clear indications of, for example, a Dutch influence in Keshy Yena, and of Spanish influence in the Salsa de Tomate. It is one of the delights when dealing with the food of this region to speculate upon the origins and adaptations of recipes by settlers so many years ago and by local inhabitants ever since.

The stuffed Edam dish is so unusual and yet so simple, adaptable and delicious that it must be the high spot of the meal. It originates in Curaçao (formerly a Dutch colony) and yet is now commonly found in Mexico as 'Queso Relleno'. The filling need not be elaborate but piquancy is needed to contrast with the flavour of the cheese. The cheese will inevitably 'run' so it should be cooked in a dish of a similar shape to the cheese. Alternatively, slices of cheese can be placed at the base and top of the dish and the filling in between. This decreases the quantity of cheese necessary and obviates the need to purchase a whole Edam, with the associated problem of how to use up the cheese from the scooped-out centre.

The great number of unusual and interesting vegetables which are used by West Indians deserved consideration when constructing this dinner party, but because of the possible difficulties in obtaining them, I have included only one dish using a vegetable which might be difficult to obtain (in your area). This is Stuffed Cho-cho; cho-cho is a pear-shaped vegetable of the squash family, sometimes called chayote or christophene depending on the country which colonized the island. It is not a wildly exciting new flavour as its flesh is akin to our vegetable marrow, but any new food is always a good talking point among your guests.

The Pumpkin curry from the French speaking island of Martinique is a delicious, lightly spiced dish which will add interest as pumpkin is a rarely used and much underrated vegetable. At certain times of the year it may be difficult to obtain pumpkin so marrow (summer squash), courgettes (zucchini) or squash may have to be substituted.

Two other interesting vegetable dishes are aubergines (eggplants) cooked in coconut cream from the Leeward Islands and okra with cornmeal from Barbados. Both are simple to prepare and the aubergine (eggplant) dish could be easily adapted. New potatoes cooked in this way are delicious (not dissimilar to 'Gratin Savoyard', substituting coconut cream for dairy cream). The Coo-coo is a traditional dish of Barbados and because of its sturdiness, it could make a meal on its own if combined with a sauce — Salsa de Tomate, for instance. Coo-coo could be made with vegetables other than okra. In the West Indies it is also made with breadfruit and sweetcorn. I would suggest asparagus or courgettes (zucchini) as alternatives, and the addition of herbs or creamed coconut could also be tried.

From Cuba in the north comes Moros y Cristianos, the renowned black beans and rice dish much enjoyed by the plantation workers when they return from their work. It is a fairly bland dish if served on its own but, where it is eaten regularly in the West Indies, the natives have many ways of spicing up plain dishes. The large range of chilli and hot pepper sauces available in this country give a clue as to how this 'spicing up' is done.

Cucumbers are rarely considered as a vegetable to be served hot, and even less to complement the flavour of oranges. Thus the Puerto Rican dish is a most unusual offering which will delight your guests with its aroma, and taste.

Plantains are another common ingredient in West Indian food. They are large, hard bananas with skins that blacken when they are ripe. The skin has to be peeled off with a knife even when black. The flesh has a pink tinge and it must be cooked before it can be eaten as it tastes extremely floury when raw. Plantains can be fried in the form of chips, curried in a spicy coconut sauce or roasted in the oven.

The two sauces complete the meal in style. The hot peppers used in the Haitian sauce and in the aubergine (eggplant) dish are small, puffy and very hot. They come in a variety of bright colours and either fresh or dried ones can be used. If you cannot find hot peppers, chillis are almost as hot and few guests will have enough taste buds intact after swallowing a mouthful of the sauce to notice the difference! As previously mentioned a range of hot sauces is available and could be used if you do not want to make the sauce up yourself. The tomato sauce is a welcome alternative to the hot sauce for those who do not want to indulge in 'liquid fire'. It will keep well in the refrigerator.

There is no natural starter to this meal, but the wide range of dishes and flavours lends itself to much flexibility when organizing courses. You could launch the meal with its spicier elements: the sauce 'Ti-Malice', Pumpkin Curry and Moros y Cristianos. The Stuffed Chochos are pleasant on their own or perhaps with the tomato sauce. My own preference for a starter would be the combination of Coo-coo and tomato sauce. The outstanding dessert dish is obviously baked bananas, and the promise of a rum *flambé* will surely persuade your guests to leave just a little room (in their stomachs) for this delight. The alternative is a selection of beautiful tropical fresh fruits such as mangoes, lychees, persimmons, guavas and passion fruit, possibly with a pineapple as a centre piece. If you cannot obtain these fruits fresh, they can all be bought tinned and combined to give a tropical fruit salad — not nearly as attractive or as much fun.

The obvious drink to accompany this meal (the recipe for which is at the end of the chapter), is a pineapple and rum punch. An interesting addition to this is sorrel, which is a bright red bud generally obtainable in January. The red fruit can be floated on the punch to make a colourful variation. Another drink which could be served at the start of the meal is Piña Colada and the recipe for this is also given.

SUGGESTED MENUS
for 6 people

Menu I	**Menu II**

Starters

| Coo-coo | Stuffed Cho-cho |
| Salsa de Tomate | |

Main Courses

Stuffed Cho-cho	Keshy Yena
Moros y Cristianos	Stewed Cucumbers
Pumpkin Curry	Aubergines in Coconut Cream
Fried Plantains	Fried Plantains
Sauce Ti-Malice	Sauce Ti-Malice
	Salsa de Tomate

Desserts

| Baked Bananas | Tropical Fruit Bowl |

A. Starters

COO-COO
Barbados

Tinned okra may be used in this dish if fresh are unobtainable, but they will not then need cooking before the cornmeal is added.

Imperial (Metric)	American
1 lb (½ kilo) okra	1 pound okra
3 pints (1½ litres) water	7½ cupsful water
Sea salt	Sea salt
1 lb (½ kilo) cornmeal	3 cupsful cornmeal
2 oz (50g) polyunsaturated margarine	¼ cupful polyunsaturated margarine

1. Wash the okra, cut off the tops and cut them diagonally into thin slices.

2. Bring the water to the boil, add the sea salt and okra and cook for 10 minutes.

3. Pour the cornmeal into the water slowly, stirring constantly, over a low heat until the mixture is thick and smooth. Then add the margarine (the same precaution should be taken as when making Polenta, i.e. use a *long* wooden spoon for stirring).

4. Cook on a low heat for 5 to 10 minutes until the mixture thickens.

5. Turn the Coo-coo into a well greased tin at least 2 in. (5cm) deep and put it in a cool place to set.

6. The Coo-coo should be set after an hour or so. Cut it out into small squares before serving.

SALSA DE TOMATE
Dominican Republic

Imperial (Metric)	American
2 × 14 oz (400g) tins tomatoes	2 medium cans tomatoes
2 bay leaves	2 bay leaves
4 tablespoonsful olive oil	4 tablespoonsful olive oil
1 tablespoonful raw cane sugar	1 tablespoonful raw cane sugar
Seasoning	Seasoning
2 cloves garlic, crushed	2 cloves garlic, crushed

1. *Purée* the tomatoes before putting them in a saucepan to cook with the bay leaves to reduce by about half.

2. Stir in the oil and the other ingredients.

3. Remove the bay leaves before serving.

STUFFED CHO-CHOS
Jamaica

If served as a starter, or as a principal dish in the main course allow one cho-cho per person. If served as a side dish, allow half a cho-cho per person.

Imperial (Metric)	American
6 cho-chos	6 cho-chos
4 tablespoonsful vegetable oil	4 tablespoonsful vegetable oil
4 medium onions, finely chopped	4 medium onions, finely chopped
2 cloves garlic, crushed	2 cloves garlic, crushed
4 oz (100g) tvp re-hydrated in red wine or stock	1 cupful tvp re-hydrated in red wine or stock
14 oz (400g) tin tomatoes	1 medium can tomatoes
1 tablespoonful chilli sauce or whole grain mustard	1 tablespoonful chilli sauce or whole grain mustard
3 tablespoonsful soya sauce	3 tablespoonsful soya sauce
Black pepper	Black pepper
4 tablespoonsful Parmesan, finely grated	4 tablespoonsful Parmesan, finely grated

1. Boil the cho-chos in salted water for 30 minutes until tender.

2. Cut the cho-chos in half lengthwise.

3. Scoop out the edible seed and then the pulp.

4. Mash the pulp.

5. Heat the oil and fry the onion and garlic until transparent.

6. Add the tvp and fry for a further 5 minutes.

7. Stir in the tomatoes and cho-cho pulp and add the seasonings including the chilli sauce or mustard depending on availability and personal taste. Cook for 10 to 15 minutes until the tvp is tender.

8. Place the filling in the cho-cho shells and sprinkle with Parmesan.

9. Bake at 350°F/180°C (Gas Mark 4) for 15 minutes until lightly browned.

B. Main Courses

PUMPKIN CURRY
Martinique

Imperial (Metric)	American
4 tablespoonsful oil	4 tablespoonsful oil
4 medium onions, finely chopped	4 medium onions, finely chopped
2 cloves garlic, crushed	2 cloves garlic, crushed
2 green peppers, chopped	2 green peppers, chopped
1 teaspoonful cloves, ground	1 teaspoonful cloves, ground
1 teaspoonful cumin seeds, ground	1 teaspoonful cumin seeds, ground
1 teaspoonful coriander seeds, ground	1 teaspoonful coriander seeds, ground
½ teaspoonful fenugreek seeds, ground	½ teaspoonful fenugreek seeds, ground
½ teaspoonful turmeric	½ teaspoonful turmeric
1 teaspoonful paprika	1 teaspoonful paprika
Sea salt	Sea salt
14 oz (400g) tin tomatoes	1 medium can tomatoes
2 lb (1 kilo) pumpkin, cut into ½ in. (1cm) cubes	2 pound pumpkin, cut into ½ in. cubes

1. Heat the oil in a heavy pan, add the onions and garlic and fry until transparent.

2. Add the peppers and fry for a further 5 minutes.

3. Add the spices and salt and stir well.

4. Add the tomatoes and pumpkin.

5. Cook on a low heat for about an hour, adding more liquid if necessary.

KESHY YENA COE TVP
Curaçao

Imperial (Metric)	American
4 oz (100g) butter	½ cupful butter
2 medium onions, finely chopped	2 medium onions, finely chopped
½ lb (¼ kilo) tvp re-hydrated in red wine	½ pound tvp re-hydrated in red wine
1 green pepper, coarsely chopped	1 green pepper, coarsely chopped
4 oz (100g) mushrooms, sliced	2 cupsful mushrooms, sliced
1 tablespoonful chilli sauce	1 tablespoonful chilli sauce
2 tablespoonsful brandy	2 tablespoonsful brandy
3 tablespoonsful tomato *purée*	3 tablespoonsful tomato paste
2 hard-boiled eggs, sliced	2 hard-boiled eggs, sliced
2 tablespoonsful raisins	2 tablespoonsful raisins
3 tablespoonsful black olives, stoned and chopped	3 tablespoonsful black olives, stoned and chopped
2 tablespoonsful capers	2 tablespoonsful capers
1 tablespoonful vinegar	1 tablespoonful vinegar
2 tablespoonsful *Holbrook's* Worcestershire sauce	2 tablespoonsful *Holbrook's* Worcestershire sauce
Seasoning	Seasoning
1 Edam cheese, usually about 4 lb (2 kilo) in weight	1 Edam cheese, usually about 4 pounds in weight

1. Heat the butter and fry the onions until golden.

2. Add the tvp and fry for 10 minutes.

3. Add the pepper and mushrooms and cook for a further 5 minutes.

4. Add the rest of the ingredients for the filling and mix well.

5. Cut the outer red wax covering from the cheese. Cut the top off and carefully hollow out the cheese leaving a shell ½ in. (1cm) thick.

6. If you like, add some of the cheese, grated, to the tvp mixture and fill the cheese shell with it. Replace the lid.

7. Bake in an uncovered greased casserole at 350°F/180°C (Gas Mark 4) for 30 minutes and serve immediately as the cheese will become leathery if it stands too long.

AUBERGINES IN COCONUT CREAM
Leeward Islands

Imperial (Metric)	American
2 large aubergines	2 large eggplants
1 medium onion, thinly sliced	1 medium onion, thinly sliced
1 hot red pepper, finely chopped	1 hot red pepper, finely chopped
2 oz (50g) Parmesan	2 ounces Parmesan
Seasoning	Seasoning
7 oz (200g) block coconut cream	7 ounce block coconut cream

1. Slice the aubergines (eggplants) thinly. You can salt them and allow some of the bitter juices to flow out before you rinse and use them.

2. Arrange layers of aubergines (eggplants), onions, peppers, Parmesan and seasoning in a greased ovenproof dish.

3. Meanwhile, melt the coconut cream in about 2 pints (1 litre) of water and stir until it is smooth.

4. Pour the coconut cream over the aubergines (eggplants).

5. Bake at 350°F/180°C (Gas Mark 4) for about an hour, covered, or until the aubergines (eggplants) are tender.

MOROS Y CRISTIANOS
Cuba

If black beans are unobtainable, use red kidney beans.

Imperial (Metric)	American
2 cloves garlic, crushed	2 cloves garlic, crushed
3 medium onions, finely chopped	3 medium onions, finely chopped
1 lb (½ kilo) black beans (boiled until tender)	2½ cupsful black beans (boiled until tender)
1 lb (½ kilo) long-grain brown rice, cooked	2½ cupsful long-grain brown rice, cooked
Seasoning	Seasoning
3 tablespoonsful olive oil	3 tablespoonsful olive oil
Parsley or chives to garnish	Parsley or chives to garnish

1. Fry the garlic and onion in the oil until transparent.

2. Add the other ingredients, mix well and heat through thoroughly, stirring frequently.

3. Decorate with finely chopped parsley or chives.

FRIED PLANTAINS
Jamaica

Imperial (Metric)	American
3 lb (1½ kilos) plantains	3 pounds plantains
Sea salt	Sea salt
Vegetable oil for frying	Vegetable oil for frying

1. Peel the plantains and cut into eight by quartering lengthwise and by cutting across.

2. Sprinkle with salt and leave for 15 minutes.

3. Fry in the oil until brown — this will take about 15 minutes. Start off with about 4 tablespoonsful of vegetable oil and add more if necessary.

STEWED BABY CUCUMBERS IN ORANGE SAUCE
Puerto Rico

Imperial (Metric)
2 lb (1 kilo) baby cucumbers
2 oz (50g) butter
2 tablespoonsful wholemeal flour
½ pint (¼ litre) orange juice
Sea salt
Black pepper
Grated rind of 1 orange
Cinnamon (optional)

American
2 pounds baby cucumbers
4 tablespoonsful butter
2 tablespoonsful wholewheat flour
1⅓ cupsful orange juice
Sea salt
Black pepper
Grated rind of 1 orange
Cinnamon (optional)

1. Peel the cucumbers thinly and cut in half lengthwise.

2. Scrape out the seeds carefully with a teaspoon and cut into 1 in. (2cm) long slices.

3. Drop the cucumber pieces into boiling salted water and cook for 5 minutes or so until tender. Then drain the cucumber and place into a warmed serving dish.

4. Meanwhile melt the butter in a pan and add the flour to make a roux.

5. Slowly add the orange juice and season well.

6. Add the orange rind and cook until well mixed and thick.

7. Pour the sauce over the cucumbers.

8. Sprinkle a little cinnamon powder on just before serving if you wish.

Note: These baby cucumbers, not courgettes (zucchini), are desirable for this dish as they are firmer than the normal salad cucumber. They can be obtained from oriental food shops but if you cannot find any, try using long cucumbers.

SAUCE TI-MALICE
Haiti

Imperial (Metric)
4 medium onions, finely chopped
6 tablespoonsful lime or lemon juice
4 cloves garlic, crushed
3 hot red peppers, finely chopped
Seasoning
6 tablespoonsful olive oil

American
4 medium onions, finely chopped
6 tablespoonsful lime or lemon juice
4 cloves garlic, crushed
3 hot red peppers, finely chopped
Seasoning
6 tablespoonsful olive oil

1. Soak the onions in the lime juice for about 1 hour.

2. Put them in a saucepan with the other ingredients and bring to the boil.

3. Remove from the heat and serve hot or cold.

Note: Other ingredients which could be used to vary this dish include wine vinegar, tomatoes, raw cane sugar and herbs such as oregano.

C. Dessert

BAKED BANANAS

Imperial (Metric)	American
2 lb (1 kilo) ripe bananas	2 pounds ripe bananas
2 oz (50g) butter	4 tablespoonsful butter
2 oz (50g) Demerara sugar	4 tablespoonsful Demerara sugar
1 teaspoonful honey	1 teaspoonful honey
2 tablespoonsful lemon juice	2 tablespoonsful lemon juice
2 tablespoonsful rum	2 tablespoonsful rum
½ pint (¼ litre) double cream, whipped	1⅓ cupsful heavy cream, whipped

1. Quarter the bananas by slicing lengthwise and across.

2. Add the butter, Demerara sugar, honey and lemon juice.

3. Bake uncovered at 400°F/200°C (Gas Mark 6) for 15 minutes, basting after 10 minutes.

4. Pour the rum over the bananas and, if you wish, set them on fire.

5. Hand round whipped cream with the bananas.

Note: You could vary this dish by using orange juice or lime juice instead of lemon juice.

D. Drinks

PINEAPPLE PUNCH

Imperial (Metric)	American
1 pineapple	1 pineapple
1 bottle white rum	1 bottle white rum
2 pints (1 litre) pineapple juice	5 cupsful pineapple juice
1 teaspoonful Angostura bitters	1 teaspoonful Angostura bitters

1. Peel the pineapple carefully and dice into ½ in. (1cm) cubes.

2. Soak the pineapple in the rum for about 2 hours.

3. Add the other ingredients and sample.

PIÑA COLADA

Imperial (Metric)	American
2 pints (1 litre) pineapple juice	5 cupsful pineapple juice
7 oz (200g) block creamed coconut, chopped	7 ounce block creamed coconut, chopped
1 bottle white rum	1 bottle white rum
Ice	Ice

1. Place all the ingredients in a blender and blend until well mixed.

2. Serve in tumblers.

Note: A mixer base can now be bought for this drink and can be used most successfully.

4.

GREECE

The Greek civilization was flourishing in 500 BC and with it came a growing awareness of how to eat and live well. This was eventually passed on to the Romans. However, the subsequent invasion and occupation of Greece by various nations caused the decline of Greek culinary art. In its place came a cuisine similar to that of countries to the east, such as Turkey. For this reason, the choice of dishes for this chapter and for that of Chapter 6 on Middle Eastern Food was somewhat arbitrary. Pitta bread and hummus, for example, are commonly eaten in Greece and would not be out of place as a starter for this dinner party.

Fresh vegetables widely available in Greece include tomatoes, peppers, okra, courgettes (zucchini), aubergines (eggplants) and cauliflowers. Olives are grown in abundance and they yield a thick, green olive oil which has more flavour than Italian olive oil. Lemons also are grown all over the country and they are essential to Greek cooking.

The national drink is ouzo, a spirit flavoured with aniseed. It is normally mixed with water and it could be used as an aperitif with this meal. The best known of the Greek wines is retsina which has few devotees outside Greece because its resin flavour is definitely an acquired taste.

The dishes in this chapter can be arranged in many ways in three or more courses and, as previously stated, dishes from the Middle Eastern chapter can be substituted to widen the choice, as the style of food is very much the same. My own choice would be to start off with a combination of the Chick Pea (garbanzo bean) *Purée*, Stewed

Artichoke Hearts, or Stuffed Cabbage Leaves, following up with a main course of Moussaka, mushrooms, okra and courgettes (zucchini). After all this, there is no finer dessert than fresh figs and halva, a Greek confectionery which can be obtained in a variety of flavours. Alternatively, green figs in syrup are available in tins.

The Chick Pea (garbanzo bean) *Purée* should not, of course, be served at the same meal as Hummus but it could be accompanied by pitta bread rather than garnished with croûtons. It is the herbs which can be gaily added to this dish which distinguish its flavour from that of hummus, but its consistency is due to the generous amount of olive oil which is used here. It can be served with wholemeal bread and a mixed salad as a perfectly nutritionally balanced meal and in this combination is most suitable for picnics.

The Stewed Artichoke Hearts also make an excellent starter. It is a fairly substantial vegetable dish as potatoes and onions are cooked, along with the artichoke hearts, in a fragrant sauce flavoured heavily with lemon juice. Other vegetables such as cauliflower florets and new carrots could be cooked in this way, as well as, or instead of, the artichokes.

Stuffed vine leaves are a favourite Greek delicacy and, although vine leaves can be purchased in some delicatessens and supermarkets in this country, cabbage leaves are just as good. It is convenient that the tougher, outer leaves are more suitable for this dish, leaving the heart of the cabbage for later use in salads or for stir-frying. The filling for the cabbage leaves can be varied considerably. For instance, try using millet instead of rice, or add a few mushrooms. Cabbage leaves can be stuffed with a vegetable curry and cooked in a similar way for inclusion in a Far Eastern style meal.

Moussaka is probably the best known of all Greek dishes, yet its name is an Arabic one. However, it is most likely that the invading Turks learnt the recipe for this dish from the Greeks and gave it their own name. A vegetarian version of Moussaka using textured vegetable protein is easy to prepare, and it will impress even those amongst your guests who are more familiar with the minced lamb version. Rather than use tvp you may prefer chick pea (garbanzo bean) *purée* or lentils in the layers between the aubergines (eggplants). The virtue of any layer dish is that the layers can be varied considerably and several other vegetables could be used if you do not like, or cannot obtain, aubergines (eggplants): for instance, courgettes (zucchini), new potatoes or spinach.

The final three dishes are intended simply as vegetable accompaniments to the Moussaka. The okra cooked in this way are tasty and will interest your guests as they will probably have had okra only in Indian dishes.

The mushrooms cooked in olive oil should still be firm when they are served so you must obtain fresh button mushrooms and cook them only briefly. The delicate flavours will be much appreciated by your guests whether you serve the dish as the first course or to accompany the Moussaka.

Courgettes (zucchini) are widely used in Greece so it would have been inappropriate to have omitted them as an ingredient in this dinner party. The Baked Courgettes (zucchini) recipe given here will ensure that best use is made of your oven as it can be cooked with the Moussaka and Stuffed Cabbage Leaves; all three dishes are cooked in a moderate oven.

I have mentioned Greek drinks. Personally, I favour a white wine such as Liebfraumilch with the first course and Beaujolais is most suitable with the Moussaka.

SUGGESTED MENUS
for 6 people

Menu I	Menu II

Starters

Chick Pea Purée	Stewed Artichoke Hearts
Stuffed Cabbage Leaves	Stuffed Cabbage Leaves

Main Courses

Moussaka	Moussaka
Okra	Mushrooms
Baked Courgettes	Baked Courgettes

Desserts

Green Figs Preserved	Fresh Figs
in Raw Cane Syrup	Halva

A. Starters

STEWED ARTICHOKE HEARTS

Imperial (Metric)
2 medium onions, finely chopped
¼ pint (150ml) olive oil
1 tablespoonful wholemeal flour
Juice of 2 lemons
4 oz (100g) shallots
1 lb (½ kilo) small, round new potatoes
2 × 14 oz (400g) tins artichoke hearts
1 teaspoonful dill
Seasoning

American
2 medium onions, finely chopped
⅔ cupful olive oil
1 tablespoonful wholewheat flour
Juice of 2 lemons
4 ounces shallots
1 pound small, round new potatoes
2 medium cans artichoke hearts
1 teaspoonful dill
Seasoning

1. In a wide, shallow pan (a wok would be suitable) fry the onion until transparent.

2. Add the flour slowly and stir until you have a smooth, thin roux.

3. Add the lemon juice, shallots and scrubbed new potatoes.

4. Simmer gently for 30 minutes or so until the potatoes are becoming tender. Some water may be added to cover the potatoes.

5. Drain the artichoke hearts and add them to the pan with the dill. Baste well and simmer for a further 15 minutes. The liquid should have mostly evaporated leaving a delicious, thick, lemony sauce.

Note: This dish is excellent as a starter or as a side-dish with the main course. If the dish is to be served as a starter, the artichokes should be basted once more and allowed to cool. If the dish is to be served as part of the main course, you may prefer to serve it hot.

STUFFED CABBAGE LEAVES

Although vine leaves are traditionally used in this Greek recipe, cabbage leaves make an excellent substitute. Packets of vine leaves can be bought in many delicatessens. You should try them and decide whether you prefer their flavour to that of the cabbage leaves.

Imperial (Metric)	American
About 12 cabbage leaves	About 12 cabbage leaves
4 oz (100g) long-grain brown rice	½ cupful long-grain brown rice
1 medium onion, finely chopped	1 medium onion, finely chopped
2 cloves garlic, crushed	2 cloves garlic, crushed
2 tablespoonsful olive oil	2 tablespoonsful olive oil
1 teaspoonful oregano	1 teaspoonful oregano
1 teaspoonful dill	1 teaspoonful dill
Juice of 1 lemon	Juice of 1 lemon
1 tablespoonful tomato *purée*	1 tablespoonful tomato paste
1 tablespoonful almonds, blanched	1 tablespoonful almonds, blanched
1 tablespoonful Parmesan, finely grated	1 tablespoonful Parmesan, finely grated

1. Carefully strip the leaves from the cabbage and wash them. The outer leaves are more suitable for stuffing and there is no shortage of uses for the crisp heart of the cabbage.

2. Blanch the cabbage leaves to make them pliable by dropping them into boiling water for 2 minutes.

3. Cook the rice in boiling water for about 30 minutes until it is tender and then drain it.

4. Fry the onion and garlic in the olive oil for a minute.

5. Add the rice and the other ingredients. Continue to cook for 5 minutes on a low heat, stirring frequently.

6. Allow the filling to cool before stuffing the cabbage leaves: first, use a pair of scissors to cut out a section of the tough leaf stem. Put a level tablespoonful of the filling on the leaf at the top of your cut. Fold the leaf to the centre before tucking in the sides.

Then roll up the leaf making a neat, tight package.

7. Pack the cabbage leaves tightly into a casserole, pour over them 2 tablespoonsful of olive oil, and bake at 350°F/180°C (Gas Mark 4) for about 40 minutes, or until tender.

Note: The dish can be flavoured further by placing garlic cloves, bay leaves, lemon slices and pieces of cinnamon between the cabbage rolls while it is in the oven. To prevent the cabbage leaves drying up, you can baste them from time to time and moisten them with lemon juice or water.

CHICK PEA PURÉE

This Greek dish is also very popular among the poorer people in Turkey and the Lebanon. The quantities of herbs and olive oil can be varied, but it is these ingredients, along with the garlic, which give this dish its distinctive flavour.

Imperial (Metric)	American
1 lb (½ kilo) chick peas	2 cupsful garbanzo beans
4 medium onions, finely chopped	4 medium onions, finely chopped
5 cloves garlic, crushed	5 cloves garlic, crushed
Approx. ½ pint (¼ litre) olive oil	Approx. 1⅓ cupsful olive oil
5 tablespoonsful parsley, finely chopped	5 tablespoonsful parsley, finely chopped
2 tablespoonsful dried mint or 4 tablespoonsful fresh mint	2 tablespoonsful dried mint or 4 tablespoonsful fresh mint
Juice of 2 lemons	Juice of 2 lemons
Sea salt and black pepper	Sea salt and black pepper
Croûtons	Croûtons

1. Boil the chick peas (garbanzo beans) until tender.

2. Drain the chick peas (garbanzo beans) and, when they have cooled, mince them or mash them to a *purée*.

3. Fry the onions and garlic in a little olive oil until they become transparent.

4. Add the other ingredients and heat through. Use as much olive oil as is needed to give the dish the required consistency. This is largely a matter of personal taste and it will depend on whether the dish is to be used as a dip or as a side-dish to the main course.

5. Garnish with croûtons or use as a dip with pitta or wholemeal bread.

Note: There are various other ways of serving this dish. It is excellent hot or cold and it combines particularly well with a crisp, green salad. It may be garnished with paprika and Cacik (page 103) may be poured over the chick peas (garbanzo beans) before they are served.

B. Main Courses

OKRA WITH TOMATOES AND ONIONS

Imperial (Metric)
2 lb (1 kilo) fresh okra
4 tablespoonsful olive oil
2 medium onions, finely chopped
2 × 14 oz (400g) tins tomatoes
1 tablespoonful dried marjoram
2 tablespoonsful wine vinegar
1 teaspoonful raw cane sugar
Seasoning

American
2 pounds fresh okra
4 tablespoonsful olive oil
2 medium onions, finely chopped
2 medium cans tomatoes
1 tablespoonful dried marjoram
2 tablespoonsful wine vinegar
1 teaspoonful raw cane sugar
Seasoning

1. Wash and scrub the okra. Cut off the stems and any tough skin.

2. Heat the oil in a large, wide pan. Fry the onions until transparent.

3. Add the okra and continue to fry until they are beginning to soften.

4. Add the tomatoes, marjoram, vinegar, raw cane sugar and sea salt and pepper.

5. Cook on a very low heat for 30 minutes.

Note: You may prefer to flavour this dish with coriander (cilantro) rather than with marjoram. It can be served cold but I prefer to serve it hot.

MOUSSAKA

Imperial (Metric)	American
2 lb (1 kilo) aubergines	2 pounds eggplants
6 tablespoonsful olive oil (or more)	6 tablespoonsful olive oil (or more)
1 oz (25g) butter	2½ tablespoonsful butter
1 medium onion, finely chopped	1 medium onion, finely chopped
4 cloves garlic, crushed	4 cloves garlic, crushed
6 oz (150g) tvp, re-hydrated in red wine	1½ cupsful tvp, re-hydrated in red wine
14 oz (400g) tin tomatoes	1 medium can tomatoes
1 tablespoonful oregano	1 tablespoonful oregano
2 tablespoonsful parsley, finely chopped	2 tablespoonsful parsley, finely chopped
1 teaspoonful ground nutmeg	1 teaspoonful ground nutmeg
Seasoning	Seasoning
¼ pint (150ml) vegetable stock	⅔ cupful vegetable stock
4 oz (100g) tomato *purée*	⅔ cupful tomato paste
2 eggs	2 eggs
¼ pint (150ml) single cream	⅔ cupful light cream
6 tablespoonsful Parmesan, finely grated	6 tablespoonsful Parmesan, finely grated

1. Slice the aubergines (eggplants) fairly thinly, put them in a colander, sprinkle with sea salt and allow to stand for 30 minutes. Rinse and dry the slices.

2. Fry the aubergine (eggplant) slices in olive oil until browned on both sides. Drain on absorbent paper and put aside.

3. Melt the butter and fry the onion and garlic until transparent.

4. Add the tvp and the tomatoes along with the oregano, parsley and nutmeg. Season well with sea salt and black pepper.

5. Simmer for 20 to 30 minutes, adding more liquid if necessary.

6. Grease a casserole dish and arrange in it alternate layers of aubergine (eggplant) and tvp, starting and finishing with aubergines (eggplants). Sprinkle each layer with a tablespoonful of Parmesan.

7. Combine the tomato *purée* and stock and pour this into the casserole.

8. Bake in a moderate oven, at 350°F/180°C (Gas Mark 4) for about 30 minutes.

9. Meanwhile blend the eggs and cream and season with sea salt and pepper.

10. Pour this mixture over the dish and sprinkle with the remaining Parmesan and bake for a further 15 to 20 minutes until the sauce is set and golden brown.

MUSHROOMS IN OLIVE OIL

Imperial (Metric)	American
2 lb (1 kilo) button mushrooms	8 cupsful button mushrooms
¼ pint (150ml) olive oil	⅔ cupful olive oil
3 tablespoonsful dry white wine	3 tablespoonsful dry white wine
Juice of 2 lemons	Juice of 2 lemons
2 teaspoonsful thyme	2 teaspoonsful thyme
5 cloves garlic, crushed	5 cloves garlic, crushed
2 oz (50g) parsley, finely chopped	2 cupsful parsley, finely chopped

1. Wash and dry the mushrooms. Cut any larger ones in half.

2. Pour the oil and wine into a pan and stir in all the ingredients except the mushrooms.

3. Bring this to the boil before adding the mushrooms. Simmer for 10 minutes.

4. Chill before serving.

BAKED COURGETTES

Imperial (Metric)	American
2 lb (1 kilo) courgettes, sliced	2 pounds zucchini, sliced
1 medium onion, thinly sliced	1 medium onion, thinly sliced
14 oz (400g) tin tomatoes	1 medium can tomatoes
6 tablespoonful olive oil	6 tablespoonful olive oil
6 tablespoonful vegetable stock	6 tablespoonful vegetable stock
1 teaspoonful raw cane sugar	1 teaspoonful raw cane sugar
2 cloves garlic, crushed	2 cloves garlic, crushed
2 tablespoonful parsley, finely chopped	2 tablespoonful parsley, finely chopped
Seasoning	Seasoning
2 tablespoonful breadcrumbs	2 tablespoonful breadcrumbs
2 oz (50g) large, black olives	2 ounces large, black olives

1. Grease a casserole dish and put a layer of courgettes (zucchini) in the bottom.

2. Put in a layer of sliced onion followed by tomatoes and continue in this way until all the vegetables are used up.

3. Mix together 4 tablespoonsful of olive oil, stock, sugar, garlic and parsley and season well with sea salt and freshly ground black pepper. Pour this mixture over the vegetables.

4. Sprinkle with breadcrumbs, pour over the rest of the oil and bake in a moderate oven at 350°F/180°C (Gas Mark 4) for 1 hour.

5. Garnish with black olives.

Note: Sliced new potatoes, aubergines (eggplants) and peppers can also be used to make up the layers in this dish.

5.

FRANCE

France could justifiably claim to be the world's gastronomic leader, so it is no surprise that a delicious vegetarian dinner party can be given using a range of provincial French dishes.

It is the regional variation that makes French cooking so interesting. Her geographical position has enabled her to benefit from skills learned from people of various cultures during the course of history: since the Romans invaded France she has continued to learn from merchants from Italy and the Middle East, while through the Mediterranean, a main trade route of the world, have passed spices and fruits from the Near and Far East. The French have shown the rest of the world how to use these ingredients to good effect.

The climatic variation has contributed towards the different regions having built up their cuisine with great diversity. The French Riviera, blessed with hot, dry summers, is abundant in fruits, olives and herbs, while in the North there is a range of ingredients more familiar to us in the British Isles: onions, chestnuts, apples and the famous soft cheeses, Brie and Camembert. All round France are centres of great wine production: Burgundy in the East produces my favourite white wine, while Bordeaux in the West produces excellent red wine. Cognac, Cointreau, Cassis, and Calvados are other great products of French ingenuity, while in the Vosges is produced that superb liqueur, Kirsch, much used in fruit desserts and fondues.

Several of the dishes could effectively be used as starters. My choice would be either the Stuffed Tomatoes and Aubergine Galette, or the Vegetable Salad, possibly served with a wholemeal roll. These dishes, if not used as starters, would be equally effective as main course side dishes. The quiches are the centre piece of the main course, but the superb vegetable dishes make this meal such a delight. A lavish dessert is the Chocolate Mousse originating in the Basque area. Much simpler but equally appropriate is an array of French cheeses such as Brie, Roquefort, Camembert, St Paulin and Tome au Raisin.

Regional contrasts of cuisine are well illustrated by the two quiches or flans which form the main dishes of the dinner party. The Quiche Niçoise from the South splendidly combines the olives, tomatoes, herbs, garlic and cheese of the area and is closely related to the local Pissaladière. Blue cheese may seem a somewhat unusual ingredient, but it gives the quiche a superb flavour and, incidentally, it is made a short way to the north in Auvergne. Dolcelatte is my favourite blue cheese for this recipe, though any will do.

The classic onion tart from Alsace on the border with Germany is also known as Zewelwaï. Its creaminess contrasts with the aromatic southern quiche while its richness is appropriate as Alsace is among the most agriculturally fertile and industrially productive regions of France.

The Stuffed Tomato dish is easy to prepare yet is delicious and brings an air of luxury to any meal. It is particularly appropriate when tomatoes are cheap, and several extra portions could be made at such a time and deep-frozen for future use. The onion dish from Monaco is best made with shallots and is a traditional way of poaching the vegetable in the South-East of France. It may soon become a favourite dish in your dinner party repertoire.

From Charente and Poitou in the West come cereals, truffles and vines. It is an area in which much brandy is made (and drunk) and many varieties of beans are grown. Not surprisingly, red wine and brandy are ingredients of the tasty dish I have chosen from the region; a baked bean dish which is most popular with children.

There are many superb southern French aubergine (eggplant) dishes that could be included here and I was particularly tempted to use Aubergines à la Bordelaise in which the aubergines (eggplants) are *sautéed* with garlic, topped with breadcrumbs and then baked. However, the galette is a dish which is prepared well in advance and is a most glamorous presentation.

To offset the richness of the rest of the meal, it is a good idea to include a salad, and the basic mixed vegetable salad is similar to a Russian salad and can be prepared well in advance and kept chilled. The ingredients can be varied according to season and personal taste, and the dish could be made into a course of its own, perhaps as an appetizer with the red cabbage dish.

There are many ways of cooking red cabbage; it is particularly good with chestnuts, or, more commonly, with apples and onions. The dish included here originates both from Les Landes, the marshy tracts of Gascony, and from the Flemish parts of France: Artois, Flanders and Picardy. Common to all recipes for red cabbage is a long, slow cooking period. To ease the pressure on the available oven space, I would suggest that you use the cooker top for this dish.

The meal is completed with one of the many famous French potato dishes. Several such dishes come from the South-East of France (Savoy, Dauphiné and Auvergne). The Gratin Dauphinois is less elaborate than the Gratin Savoyard, because it is just a dish of thinly sliced potatoes cooked in cream or milk with butter and seasoning, baked in a medium oven for about an hour, or until the potatoes are cooked. The Gratin Savoyard uses Gruyère cheese (or Beaufort, the local cheese) and a variety of other ingredients which may include milk, cream or stock, grated onions, mushrooms, eggs, various herbs and breadcrumbs. Whichever way you combine the ingredients, you will find this a very popular dish with your guests.

Whole books have been written about French wine, so I shall mention only the wines which I know have been enjoyably consumed as an accompaniment to this meal. I have already mentioned White Burgundy, and Macon Blanc and Muscadet are both excellent white wines. A red wine is less appropriate but with areas such as Beaujolais, Burgundy and Bordeaux from which to choose a wine, there should be no problem in finding a suitable accompaniment if you should want to offer red wine.

SUGGESTED MENUS
for 6 people

Menu I	Menu II
Starters	
French Vegetable Salad	Aubergine Galette
Main Courses	
Quiche Niçoise	Tarte à l'Oignon Alsacienne
Haricots à la Charente	Oignons à la Monégasque
Gratin Savoyard	Chou Rouge à la Flamande
Tomates Farcies Provençales	Gratin Savoyard
Desserts	
Mousse au Chocolat	French Cheese Board
	Biscuits for cheese

A. Starters

TOMATES FARCIES PROVENÇALES

This dish is simple to prepare, yet is a most tasty part of the meal. More elaborate forms of this dish would include mushrooms, a variety of herbs or an egg in the filling.

Imperial (Metric)	American
1½ lb (¾ kilo) large, firm tomatoes	1½ pounds large, firm tomatoes
1 tablespoonful basil, dried	1 tablespoonful basil, dried
2 cloves garlic, crushed	2 cloves garlic, crushed
1 tablespoonful thyme, finely chopped	1 tablespoonful thyme, finely chopped
4 oz (100g) wholemeal breadcrumbs	2 cupsful wholewheat breadcrumbs
2 medium onions, finely chopped	2 medium onions, finely chopped
Seasoning	Seasoning
3 tablespoonsful olive oil	3 tablespoonsful olive oil

1. Cut the tops off the tomatoes and reserve them. Scoop out the pulp using a teaspoon. Invert the empty shells to drain thoroughly.

2. Combine the tomato pulp with the other ingredients except the olive oil and mix well to make a thick paste.

3. Fill the tomatoes and replace their tops.

4. Put the tomatoes in a baking dish with the olive oil and baste each one.

5. Bake for 30 minutes at 400°F/200°C (Gas Mark 6) basting occasionally.

AUBERGINE GALETTE

Imperial (Metric)	American
1 lb (½ kilo) aubergines	1 pound eggplants
Sea salt	Sea salt
About ¼ pint (150ml) olive oil	⅔ cupful olive oil
1 medium onion, finely chopped	1 medium onion, finely chopped
1 clove garlic, crushed	1 clove garlic, crushed
14 oz (400g) tin tomatoes	1 medium can tomatoes
¼ pint (150ml) yogurt	⅔ cupful yogurt

1. Slice the aubergines (eggplants) into ½ in. (1cm) slices and sprinkle with sea salt. Leave for 30 minutes.

2. Rinse and dry the aubergine (eggplant) slices.

3. Heat the oil and fry the slices until brown.

4. Fry the onion and garlic in some olive oil. After a few minutes add the tomatoes (but not the juice).

5. In a round, deep, oven-proof dish place alternate layers of aubergines (eggplants), tomatoes and onions and yogurt.

6. Leave for a day and then bake in a moderate oven at 350°F/180°C (Gas Mark 4) for 45 minutes.

7. Allow to cool before turning out. A suitable garnish would be fresh herbs.

Note: I have successfully made this dish using ground cashew nuts in layers instead of the yogurt. If you turn the galette out too long before the meal it may spread so I would recommend that you turn it out just before serving.

FRENCH VEGETABLE SALAD

Imperial (Metric)	American
1 lb (½ kilo) new potatoes	1 pound new potatoes
1 lb (½ kilo) carrots, scraped	1 pound carrots, scraped
½ lb (¼ kilo) fresh green beans	½ pound fresh green beans
½ lb (¼ kilo) peas	1⅓ cupsful peas
1 cauliflower	1 cauliflower
1 large cucumber	1 large cucumber
Vinaigrette dressing (see below)	Vinaigrette dressing (see below)
Chopped parsley	Chopped parsley
4 tablespoonsful capers	4 tablespoonsful capers

1. Cook the potatoes and carrots in boiling salted water until tender.

2. Put the potatoes into cold water before peeling them carefully. Dice the potatoes and carrots into small cubes.

3. Cook the beans and peas in boiling water for a short time.

4. Cook the cauliflower florets in the same way in boiling water for a short time. They should still be crisp.

5. Peel the cucumber thinly and dice it.

6. Arrange the vegetables attractively on a tray and season well with vinaigrette dressing.

7. Chill well and garnish with parsley and capers.

VINAIGRETTE

Imperial (Metric)	American
4 tablespoonsful white wine vinegar	4 tablespoonsful white wine vinegar
2 tablespoonsful lemon juice	2 tablespoonsful lemon juice
1 tablespoonful wholegrain mustard	1 tablespoonful wholegrain mustard
Sea salt and black pepper	Sea salt and black pepper
6 tablespoonsful olive oil	6 tablespoonsful olive oil
1 tablespoonful honey	1 tablespoonful honey
1 clove garlic, crushed	1 clove garlic, crushed

Mix all the ingredients well, preferably in a blender.

B. Main Courses

QUICHE NIÇOISE

Imperial (Metric)	American
½ lb (¼ kilo) wholemeal flour	2 cupsful wholewheat flour
4 oz (100g) vegetable margarine	½ cupful vegetable margarine
Sea salt	Sea salt
1 medium onion, finely chopped	1 medium onion, finely chopped
2 cloves garlic, crushed	2 cloves garlic, crushed
Olive oil	Olive oil
14 oz (400g) tin tomatoes	1 medium can tomatoes
1 teaspoonful basil	1 teaspoonful basil
1 teaspoonful oregano	1 teaspoonful oregano
4 oz (100g) blue cheese	½ cupful blue cheese
4 eggs, beaten	4 eggs, beaten
Black olives	Black olives
Parmesan cheese, finely grated	Parmesan cheese, finely grated

1. Make the shortcrust pastry by mixing well the flour and vegetable margarine with a pinch of sea salt. Add sufficient water to make a firm dough and set aside in a cool place while you make the filling.

2. Fry the onion and garlic in about 4 tablespoonsful of olive oil until they turn transparent.

3. Add the tomatoes and herbs and cook for a further 10 minutes.

4. Take the pan off of the heat and meanwhile whisk the blue cheese with the eggs until the mixture is smooth.

5. Add the cheese and eggs to the tomato mixture and mix well. You may like to season with black pepper but no extra sea salt is needed.

6. Roll out the pastry and fill a large flan tin. Cover the pastry with greaseproof paper and weigh down with a few dried beans.

7. Bake the pastry case 'blind' in a hot oven at 400°F/200°C (Gas Mark 6) for 12 minutes.

8. Fill the flan case with the mixture and decorate with the olives. Sprinkle Parmesan over the centre of the quiche.

9. Bake at 350°F/180°C (Gas Mark 4) for 30 minutes or until browning on top.

Note: A little olive oil may be poured over the quiche before it is baked to give it a shiny appearance. The quiche is delicious hot or cold.

TARTE À L'OIGNON ALSACIENNE

Imperial (Metric)	American
¾ lb (350g) shortcrust pastry (as for Quiche Niçoise)	¾ pound shortcrust pastry (as for Quiche Niçoise)
6 medium onions, thinly sliced	6 medium onions, thinly sliced
2 oz (50g) butter	4 tablespoonsful butter
4 eggs	4 eggs
½ pint (¼ litre) single cream	1⅓ cupsful cream
Seasoning	Seasoning
A few caraway seeds	A few caraway seeds

1. Make the shortcrust pastry and set aside in a cool place.

2. Fry the onions gently in the butter until they become transparent.

3. Roll out the pastry and line a large flan tin. Cover the pastry with greaseproof paper and weigh down with a few dried beans.

4. Bake the pastry case 'blind' in a hot oven at 400°F/200°C (Gas Mark 6) for 12 minutes.

5. Spread the onions over the flan case.

6. Combine the other ingredients in a blender.

7. Pour this mixture over the onions.

8. Bake at 350°F/180°C (Gas Mark 4) for 30 minutes or until browned on top.

Note: There are several variations on this recipe such as using cream cheese on top of the pie shell, so making layers of pastry, cream cheese, onion and cream topping.

OIGNONS À LA MONÉGASQUE

This is a novel way to cook small onions or shallots. You may choose to replace some of the water in the recipe with white wine, so that less water is needed to cover.

Imperial (Metric)	American
2 lb (1 kilo) small white onions or shallots	2 pounds small white onions or shallots
¼ pint (150ml) olive oil	⅔ cupful olive oil
¼ pint (150ml) white wine vinegar	⅔ cupful white wine vinegar
Water to cover	Water to cover
6 bay leaves	6 bay leaves
2 teaspoonsful marjoram	2 teaspoonsful marjoram
4 cloves garlic, crushed (optional)	4 cloves garlic, crushed (optional)
Seasoning	Seasoning
2 tablespoonsful tomato *purée*	2 tablespoonsful tomato paste
2 tablespoonsful raisins	2 tablespoonsful raisins

1. Peel the onions and place in a saucepan with the olive oil.

2. Toss the onions until all are coated with the oil.

3. Add the other ingredients.

4. Bring the onions to the boil then cook over a low heat, covered, for about 30 minutes until the onions are tender (but not soft).

5. Chill before serving.

HARICOTS À LA CHARENTE

Imperial (Metric)	American
1 lb (½ kilo) dried haricot beans	2 cupsful dried navy beans
2 medium onions	2 medium onions
4 cloves	4 cloves
3 cloves garlic	3 cloves garlic
2 bay leaves	2 bay leaves
4 tablespoonsful olive oil	4 tablespoonsful olive oil
3 sticks celery, finely chopped	3 stalks celery, finely chopped
4 oz (100g) tomato *purée*	4 ounces tomato paste
4 tablespoonsful parsley, finely chopped	4 tablespoonsful parsley, finely chopped
3 tablespoonsful brandy	3 tablespoonsful brandy
½ bottle dry red wine	½ bottle dry red wine
Seasoning	Seasoning

1. Soak the beans overnight in sufficient water to cover.

2. Pour the beans into a large pot with the onions stuck with cloves, the garlic and the bay leaves.

3. Cover with water and simmer for about 2 hours until the beans are tender.

4. Drain the beans, reserving the liquid but discarding the onions, bay leaves and garlic.

5. Fry the celery in the olive oil until transparent.

6. Add the tomato *purée*, parsley, brandy and wine.

7. Simmer to reduce this sauce by about half.

8. Put the beans into a casserole, add sea salt and black pepper and pour the sauce over them. Add enough of the reserved bean stock to cover the beans.

9. Cover the casserole and bake at 350°F/180°C (Gas Mark 4) for 2 hours.

CHOU ROUGE À LA FLAMANDE

Imperial (Metric)
4 medium onions, thinly sliced
4 cloves garlic, crushed
4 oz (100g) butter
1 small red cabbage, thinly sliced
4 cooking apples, peeled and thinly
  sliced
½ bottle red wine
⅜ pint (200ml) red wine vinegar
2 bay leaves
8 cloves
4 tablespoonsful redcurrant jelly

American
4 medium onions, thinly sliced
4 cloves garlic, crushed
½ cupful butter
1 small red cabbage, thinly sliced
4 cooking apples, peeled and thinly
  sliced
½ bottle red wine
¾ cupful red wine vinegar
2 bay leaves
8 cloves
4 tablespoonsful redcurrant jelly

1. Fry the onions and garlic in the butter for a few minutes.

2. Fill a large saucepan with alternate layers of red cabbage, apple, onion and garlic.

3. Put the other ingredients in the top and moisten with wine and wine vinegar.

4. Cook on a low heat for 2 hours or until the cabbage is tender.

Note: Fill the large saucepan to the brim as the cabbage will 'cook down' considerably over the cooking period.

GRATIN SAVOYARD

Imperial (Metric)	American
2 lb (1 kilo) new potatoes, cleaned and thinly sliced	2 pounds new potatoes, cleaned and thinly sliced
1 pint (½ litre) single cream	2½ cupsful cream
½ lb (¼ kilo) Gruyère cheese, grated	2 cupsful Gruyère cheese, grated
1 tablespoonful rosemary, finely chopped	1 tablespoonful rosemary, finely chopped
Seasoning	Seasoning
2 oz (50g) butter	4 tablespoonsful butter
6 oz (150g) breadcrumbs	3 cupsful breadcrumbs

1. Mix together the cream, cheese, seasoning and rosemary.

2. Butter a large casserole and arrange in it alternate layers of potatoes and the cream mixture, finishing with the cream mixture on the top.

3. Sprinkle with the breadcrumbs, dot with butter and cover.

4. Cook at 350°F/180°C (Gas Mark 4) for 2 hours until the potatoes are tender.

Note: You may prefer to speed up the cooking of this delicious dish by boiling the potatoes until just tender before peeling and slicing. The dish can then be cooked in half the time in the oven.

C. Dessert

MOUSSE AU CHOCOLAT

Imperial (Metric)	American
¾ lb (350g) plain chocolate	¾ pound plain chocolate
6 tablespoonsful black coffee	6 tablespoonsful black coffee
1 oz (25g) butter	2½ tablespoonsful butter
2 tablespoonsful rum	2 tablespoonsful rum
3 drops vanilla essence	3 drops vanilla essence
6 eggs, separated	6 eggs, separated
½ pint (¼ litre) double cream, whipped	1⅓ cupsful heavy cream, whipped

1. Break the chocolate into small pieces, put into a bowl with the coffee and place the bowl over a saucepan of boiling water. Stir to a thick cream.

2. Stir in the butter, rum and vanilla.

3. Remove the bowl from the heat and stir in the egg yolks. Mix well.

4. Whisk the egg whites until they are stiff.

5. Stir the beaten egg whites into the chocolate.

6. Spoon the mousse into wine glasses and put into a cool place for several hours to set.

7. Pipe whipped cream generously onto the top of the individual mousses.

6.

THE MIDDLE EAST

The culinary influence of this region extends far beyond its normally accepted geographical boundaries and it is rarely possible to ascribe a dish to a particular country. It is also true that many of the dishes in the chapter on Greek food could be interchanged with those here because of the Eastern influence which exists in Greece. The main countries in my consideration of the food of this region are Turkey, the Lebanon and Iran.

The people of the region are traditionally sociable, and they entertain with enthusiasm, so the ideas put forward in this book would meet with approval there, where it is the duty of the host to lay before his guests the best food available and the guests are expected to admire the food. I am sure that your guests will also admire the dishes in this dinner party.

Improvisation is a key ingredient in the cooking of this region and, as elsewhere, quantities and cooking times should be taken only as a guide. Many dishes are common to several countries both inside and outside the Middle East and the variations in recipes, usually minor, show also that there is no exact set of quantities for any particular dish.

I will not extol the various rituals that are practised at mealtimes, many of which were put forward by Muhammed in the Koran. The fact that alcohol is forbidden in many parts of the area suggests that there is no obvious alcoholic accompaniment to these meals, but I would suggest a dry wine of your choice.

In Arab countries, bread is eaten at virtually every meal but it is quite different from our common tin loaf. It is made flat and round, and only slightly leavened so that when cooked for a short time at a high temperature it puffs up and is consequently suitable for filling with *falafels* (fried chick pea balls), yogurt and salad. This pitta bread is also ideal for 'dunking' into dips, and there are two noted ones from this region: Hummus and Cacik. Hummus combines the highly nutritious chick pea (garbanzo bean) with sesame seed paste or tahini, which is an excellent source of calcium. Flavoured with lemon juice and garlic, it makes a perfect snack with wholemeal or pitta bread, and an ideal starter for this meal. Cacik (which can be spelt in many ways) is a refreshing cucumber, mint and yogurt dip, which, like hummus, is popular throughout the Middle East.

Although Tabbouleh is a salad, I would serve it with the main course as its fresh flavours will be appreciated here. It is a Lebanese dish made from *burghul* (or *bulgur*) which is cracked wheat, and it is flavoured with liberal quantities of mint and parsley with a little onion. It should be served decoratively on vine or lettuce leaves.

It has been said that the Turks have devised more than forty ways of cooking aubergines (eggplants). The most famous of these is Imam Bayildi, which, when translated, means 'the priest fainted'. This may have been because a Turkish priest fainted, presumably with pleasure, when his wife prepared this delightful dish! There are many other fillings for stuffed aubergines (eggplants) but this is the one which fits in best with the nutritional values and flavours of the other dishes in this course.

The Persian Empire was the first to dominate the entire region and its culinary influence is still felt. The food eaten in Iran has changed little over the centuries because of the poverty of the peasants and much of their food is still cooked over charcoal fires in the open air. The Lentil and Spinach dish was prepared in medieval Persia and served to the Persian sick. It is a highly nutritious and warming dish but you should take care to ensure that it is fairly thick when you serve it.

The final dish in the main course provides colour and contrast — a Turkish Pilaff, the ingredients of which can be varied enormously. Common local vegetables such as tomatoes, peppers and okra are used along with apricots, raisins and almonds. This is truly a king among rice dishes, and if served cold this recipe is a good basis for a rice salad.

A pleasant, rather unusual dessert is a dried fruit salad, which can be varied according to your personal tastes and the availability of the different types of dried fruit. Another refreshing dessert is Apricot Fool, using dried apricots.

SUGGESTED MENUS
for 6 people

Menu I

Menu II

Starters

Pitta Bread
Hummus
Cacik

Pitta Bread
Hummus
Cacik.

Main Courses

Turkish Pilaff
Imam Bayildi
Lentils and Spinach

Tabbouleh
Imam Bayildi
Lentils and Spinach

(Vegetable dishes to supplement may be selected from Chapter 4)

Desserts

Apricot Fool

Dried Fruit Salad

RECIPES

A. Starters

PITTA BREAD

It is possible to buy wholemeal pitta bread but there is a great satisfaction to be gained from making your own.

Imperial (Metric)	American
1 oz (25g) dried yeast	2 tablespoonsful dried yeast
1½ pints (¾ litre) lukewarm water	3¾ cupsful lukewarm water
1 tablespoonful raw cane sugar	1 tablespoonful raw cane sugar
3 lb (1½ kilos) wholemeal flour	12 cupsful wholewheat flour
2 teaspoonsful sea salt	2 teaspoonsful sea salt
5 tablespoonsful olive oil	5 tablespoonsful olive oil

1. Dissolve the yeast in about ¼ pint (150ml) of lukewarm water.

2. Add the sugar to the yeast and leave in a warm place for 10 minutes until it is frothy and bubbly.

3. Mix the flour and the sea salt.

4. Pour the yeast mixture into the flour and knead well for 10 minutes, adding enough water to make a firm dough. Gradually add the oil to the dough while you are kneading.

5. Put the dough into a large greased bowl, ensuring that the dough is greased all over.

6. Cover the bowl with a damp cloth and leave it in a warm place for 2 hours or so, by which time it should have risen to several times its original volume.

7. Take the dough from the bowl and knead for a few minutes more.

8. Take lumps of dough between 2 and 3 in. (5-7cm) in diameter.

9. By hand, or with a rolling pin, flatten each lump on a lightly floured surface until it is about 6 in. (15cm) across.

10. Lay each round of bread on a floured cloth and cover with another floured cloth. Allow to rise in a warm place.

11. Preheat the oven to 425°F/220°C (Gas Mark 7).

12. Put several oiled baking trays in the oven for a few minutes to heat through.

13. Put the bread onto the hot baking sheets.

14. Bake for about 10 minutes near the middle of the oven.

Note: This quantity will make about 25 'loaves', and those you do not eat can easily be frozen for later use.

HUMMUS

Imperial (Metric)	American
6 oz (150g) chick peas	1 cupful garbanzo beans
Juice of 3-4 lemons, to taste	Juice of 3-4 lemons, to taste
4-5 cloves garlic, to taste	4-5 cloves garlic, to taste
⅜ pint (200ml) light tahini	¾ cupful light tahini
1 teaspoonful sea salt	1 teaspoonful sea salt
2 tablespoonsful olive oil	2 tablespoonsful olive oil
½ teaspoonful paprika	½ teaspoonful paprika
Parsley or coriander loaves	Parsley or cilantro leaves

1. Boil the chick peas (garbanzo beans) for an hour or more until they become soft. Alternatively, put them in a pressure cooker and cook for 15 minutes. When the chick peas (garbanzo beans) have cooled, and if you have time, remove as many skins from them as possible.

2. The best way to *purée* the chick peas (garbanzo beans) to the required consistency is with a mincer. It is a long, arduous process with a potato masher, and the consistency is too thick to make a blender viable.

3. Add the other ingredients to the *purée*, varying the exact quantity according to your own preference. Mix well.

4. If the *pâté* is too thick (and this again is a matter of personal preference), add some water or some olive oil.

5. Put the hummus in a number of small bowls and garnish each with olive oil, paprika, parsley or coriander (cilantro) and, perhaps, a few whole chick peas (garbanzo beans).

CACIK

There are obvious similarities between this dish and the raitas in Indian cookery. Although it is an excellent side dish to accompany the main course, it is more appropriate to serve it with the pitta bread and hummus as a dip.

Imperial (Metric)	American
1 cucumber	1 cucumber
1 tablespoonful dried mint	1 tablespoonful dried mint
1 pint (½ litre) yogurt	2½ cupsful yogurt
3 cloves garlic, crushed	3 cloves garlic, crushed
Sea salt and pepper	Sea salt and pepper

1. Peel and dice the cucumber and sprinkle with salt. Drain in a colander for about 30 minutes.

2. Rinse the cucumber and allow to dry.

3. If fresh mint is available, use 3 tablespoons, finely chopped. Mix the mint into the yogurt along with the garlic, salt and pepper.

4. Add the cucumber and mix well.

5. Decorate with fresh mint or a little paprika.

B. Main Courses

IMAM BAYILDI

Imperial (Metric)	American
3 medium aubergines	3 medium eggplants
Sea salt and pepper	Sea salt and pepper
¼ pint (150ml) olive oil	⅔ cupful olive oil
2 medium onions, finely chopped	2 medium onions, finely chopped
2 cloves garlic	2 cloves garlic
14 oz (400g) tin tomatoes	1 medium can tomatoes
1 teaspoonful cinnamon, ground	1 teaspoonful cinnamon, ground
2 tablespoonsful parsley, finely chopped	2 tablespoonsful parsley, finely chopped
1 teaspoonful raw cane sugar	1 teaspoonful raw cane sugar
12 black olives	12 black olives

1. To prepare the aubergines (eggplants), remove the leaf bases.

2. Bring 2 pints (1 litre) of water to the boil in a large pan.

3. Place the aubergines (eggplants) in the pan and allow to cook for 10 minutes.

4. Remove the aubergines (eggplants) and plunge them into a pan of cold water.

5. Cut the aubergines (eggplants) in half lengthwise and carefully scoop out the inside with a spoon.

6. Sprinkle sea salt and black pepper over the aubergine (eggplant) shells and pour 2 tablespoonsful of olive oil into each shell.

7. Place the shells into an oven pre-heated to 350°F/180°C (Gas Mark 4) for 20 minutes or so while you prepare the filling.

8. Fry the onion and garlic in about 5 tablespoonsful of oil until they become transparent.

9. Drain the tomatoes and add them to the onions and garlic, along

with the cinnamon, parsley and sugar. Season with sea salt and black pepper and simmer for 10 minutes.

10. Add the chopped aubergine (eggplant) flesh and cook for a further 5 minutes or so.

11. Stuff the aubergine (eggplant) shells with the filling and garnish with black olives.

12. Return the stuffed halves to the oven for a further 10 minutes before serving. Garnish, if you wish, with finely chopped parsley.

Note: You could make this into a more substantial dish by the addition of 2 tablespoonsful of ground almonds to each aubergine (eggplant) half.

TABBOULEH

Imperial (Metric)	American
¾ lb (350g) burghul	2⅓ cupsful burghul
1 medium onion, very finely chopped	1 medium onion, very finely chopped
4 oz (100g) parsley, finely chopped	4 cupsful parsley, finely chopped
2 oz (50g) mint, finely chopped	2 cupsful mint, finely chopped
2 teaspoonsful sea salt	2 teaspoonsful sea salt
5 tablespoonsful olive oil	5 tablespoonsful olive oil
Juice of 2 lemons	Juice of 2 lemons
Vine or lettuce leaves	Vine or lettuce leaves
Lemon wedges	Lemon wedges
6 tomatoes (firm)	6 tomatoes (firm)
12 black olives	12 black olives

1. Soak the burghul in water for about 30 minutes and drain well.

2. Mix the burghul with the onion, parsley, mint, salt, olive oil and lemon juice. If you wish to season your tabbouleh, use freshly ground black pepper, cayenne pepper or cinnamon.

3. Serve on a bed of vine or lettuce leaves. Garnish the salad attractively with lemon wedges, tomato wedges and black olives.

LENTILS AND SPINACH

This Persian dish is similar to Dahl Sag — its Indian counterpart which is so popular in the north of that country. The only difference in the Persian version is the omission of spices, usually chillis, mustard seed and turmeric.

Imperial (Metric)	American
½ lb (¼ kilo) brown lentils	1 cupful brown lentils
1 lb (½ kilo) spinach	1 pound spinach
1 medium onion, finely chopped	1 medium onion, finely chopped
2 cloves garlic, crushed	2 cloves garlic, crushed
1 teaspoonful cumin seeds, ground	1 teaspoonful cumin seeds, ground
1 teaspoonful coriander seeds, ground	1 teaspoonful coriander seeds, ground
Sea salt and pepper	Sea salt and pepper
2 tablespoonsful vegetable oil	2 tablespoonsful vegetable oil
2 tablespoonsful lemon juice	2 tablespoonsful lemon juice

1. Wash the lentils and cook until tender. This will take about an hour.

2. If you are using fresh spinach, wash it and chop it finely. Put it into a saucepan with no water and cook gently and covered for about 10 minutes. If you are using frozen spinach, thaw it and drain off excess liquid before using.

3. Fry the onions and garlic in the oil until they become transparent.

4. Add the cumin and coriander and cook for a further 3 minutes.

5. Stir in the lentils and spinach and, if necessary, cook until the dish is of a fairly thick consistency.

6. Season with the salt, pepper and lemon juice.

Note: The protein value of this nutritious dish can be further increased by the addition of 2 tablespoonsful of butter just before serving and by garnishing it with hard-boiled eggs.

TURKISH PILAFF

Imperial (Metric)
2 medium onions, finely chopped
3 cloves garlic, crushed
1 lb (½ kilo) long-grain brown rice
4 tablespoonsful vegetable oil
3 bay leaves
14 oz (400g) tin tomatoes
2 tablespoonsful tomato *purée*
4 oz (100g) dried apricots
2 oz (50g) sultanas
2 oz (50g) almonds, blanched and
  shredded
Sea salt and pepper
1 pint (½ litre) stock
Coriander leaves

American
2 medium onions, finely chopped
3 cloves garlic, crushed
2 cupsful long-grain brown rice
4 tablespoonsful vegetable oil
3 bay leaves
1 medium can tomatoes
2 tablespoonsful tomato paste
¾ cupful dried apricots
⅓ cupful golden seedless raisins
½ cupful almonds, blanched and
  shredded
Sea salt and pepper
2½ cupsful stock
Cilantro

1. Fry the onions and garlic in the oil until they become transparent.

2. Add the rice and continue to fry for 3 minutes, stirring constantly.

3. Add the remaining ingredients except the coriander leaves (cilantro), bring to the boil, then simmer, covered, for 45 minutes.

4. Serve garnished with the coriander leaves (cilantro).

Note: Other ingredients which you may wish to include in this dish are saffron, fresh ginger, mushrooms, peppers, white wine (instead of some of the stock), oregano, thyme, cardamoms and cloves. Orange and lemon wedges make a colourful garnish.

C. Desserts

DRIED FRUIT SALAD

Imperial (Metric)	American
4 oz (100g) dried apricots	¾ cupful dried apricots
4 oz (100g) prunes	¾ cupful dried prunes
4 oz (100g) seedless raisins	¾ cupful raisins
4 oz (100g) figs	¾ cupful figs
4 oz (100g) dates	¾ cupful dates
4 oz (100g) almonds, blanched	¾ cupful almonds, blanched
4 oz (100g) raw cane sugar	¾ cupful raw cane sugar
2 tablespoonsful rosewater	2 tablespoonsful rosewater
2 tablespoonsful pine kernels (optional)	2 tablespoonsful pine kernels (optional)

1. Mix all the ingredients in a large bowl and cover with cold water. Allow to soak for 2 days.

2. Serve, possibly with the addition of preserved ginger and kirsch, and with whipped cream, if you wish.

APRICOT FOOL

Imperial (Metric)
¾ lb (350g) dried apricots, soaked
  overnight
Juice and rind of 1 lemon
2 tablespoonsful honey
1 pint (½ litre) yogurt
½ pint (¼ litre) double cream,
  whipped

American
2¼ cupsful dried apricots, soaked
  overnight
Juice and rind of 1 lemon
2 tablespoonsful honey
2½ cupsful yogurt
1⅓ cupsful heavy cream, whipped

1. Simmer the apricots until tender.

2. Liquidize the apricots to make a thick *purée*.

3. Add the other ingredients except the cream and liquidize.

4. Spoon into wine glasses and pipe on the whipped cream just before
   serving.

Note: Dried peaches are equally excellent in this dish.

7.

CHINA

A large number of Chinese dishes can be prepared without the use of meat or fish. The vast range of vegetables, both common and oriental, cooked in a variety of styles; the numerous ways of preparing noodles and rice; the infinite number of ways of combining these ingredients with such foods as bean curd to make ensembles; and the delicious sauces cooked in the Chinese style make this country's cuisine ideal for the basis of a vegetarian dinner party.

The greatest attraction that Chinese food has for me is its short cooking time. This means that much of the preparation for a Chinese meal is in chopping vegetables, generally into matchstick size pieces, so that they will require an equal cooking time. This process of stir-frying, by which a lot of Chinese food is cooked, ensures that much of the nutritional value of the food is preserved.

The visual appeal is important too. Short cooking does not destroy colour, and most attractive combinations can be assembled. Contrasts in texture can be created from different cooking styles: deep-fried food is crisp; stir-fried is crunchy and, depending on the sauce used, piquant; and stewed dishes are tender. Contrasts in flavour are made by varying the sauces in which the ingredients are cooked.

No special kitchen equipment is needed for Chinese cookery though a 'wok' is an advantage. A wok is a round-bottomed vessel, about 14 in. (35cm) in diameter, usually with two handles on opposite sides of the pan. There are many types available: with non-stick or non-rust finishes; with portable burners; and some with lids. If a wok is not available, an ordinary frying pan or a wide, open pan will do. A range of spatulas, stirring spoons, deep-frying baskets and skimmers are helpful and even chopsticks can be useful utensils. Of course, sharp knives are essential for all the chopping that is necessary.

White and red wines are both complementary to Chinese vegetarian food, but I have devised a superb Chinese punch which is excellent at dinner parties which you want to go with more of a swing.

The essential ingredients for Chinese cookery are generally available in supermarkets and continental food shops, but the best places to stock up are in specialist Chinese supermarkets. You will need time to familiarize yourself with the layout of the shops, but you will find the standards of service excellent.

The ideal starter for this meal is a combination of pancake rolls and the sweet-sour sauce as the range of textures and flavours is most evident in these dishes. You will find both of these dishes much tastier than their counterparts that you might find in Chinese restaurants.

You could serve the whole meal as a succession of courses just as feasts in China were organized. There is no shortage of choice of colours, textures and flavours, and also a nutritional balance which should be acceptable to even your most health-conscious guests. You should insist on the use of chopsticks as this gives more atmosphere to the meal and your guests will quickly learn how to manipulate them.

A main course should contain the Chow Mein or the Fried Rice — either are substantial dishes and need few dishes in support. I would always serve a Stir-fried Vegetable dish with this meal as this has more colour than the other dishes. The Peanut Butter Sauce will delight your guests and you can adapt it for everyday use with mixed vegetable dishes.

The meal is very filling and only a light dessert is needed; the Chinese Fruit Salad is truly luscious.

You will find that within the framework of these dishes there is the possibility of much improvisation and experimentation and, for this reason and others, you will also find that Chinese cookery is great fun.

The following notes about Chinese ingredients are intended as a guide for those people who are new to Chinese cookery and not as an exhaustive list of Chinese vegetarian ingredients.

Ingredients Used in Chinese Cookery

Bamboo Shoots — you will rarely be able to buy this pale yellow, fibrous vegetable fresh but tinned ones are excellent and quite reasonably priced. They are preserved in water either in chunks or cut into matchstick-size pieces (marked 'strip' on the tin) which can be used after draining. Braised bamboo shoots, slivered, which are more expensive, are also available as are dried bamboo shoots which must be well soaked in warm water before use.

Bean Curd (Tofu) — this is available in most Chinese supermarkets where it is kept chilled in water in chunks of about 3 in. (7cm) square by 1 in. (2cm) deep. It is white, slightly spongy and not unlike cheese in texture though bland in taste. It can be deep-fried or sliced and combined with most other ingredients. It can also be bought dried in fibrous lengths which must be well soaked before use and then it can be used with vegetable dishes or fried on its own. Both of these forms of bean curd are highly nutritious, but I would advise you against some tinned and bottled tofus which are often very salty.

Beansprouts — these are grown from tiny green mung beans. They can easily be sprouted at home in a large jar or special sprouter jar, but they are so cheap to buy that the effort of growing your own beansprouts is not really worth while unless you cannot obtain them locally. In an emergency you could use tinned beansprouts though they are not crisp like fresh beansprouts.

Chilli Sauce — there are several makes of chilli sauce available. It can be used to pour onto food directly or it can be added to a sauce to make it spicier. In any case, it must be used sparingly for obvious reasons.

Hoisin Sauce — this is also called barbecue sauce and is available in tins or glass jars. It is dark and thick with a sweet and slightly spicy flavour though its base is fermented soya beans. It can be used fairly liberally in sauces.

Lily Buds (golden needles) — the Chinese do not use the herbs with which we are familiar such as mint, thyme, basil and sage and I suppose that lily buds are the closest likeness to herbs found in Chinese recipes. They are about 2 in. (5cm) long, dried and rather sweet in taste. They should be soaked before being used in noodle or rice dishes, or before being stir-fried with vegetables.

Lotus Roots — this fibrous root is available tinned or dried and is, when tinned, pink and in chunks much like bamboo shoots. It is soft in texture, not unlike carrots when they are cooked. It should be sliced before being cooked as a part of a vegetable dish or with rice.

Mushrooms — dried Chinese mushrooms are available in all Chinese food shops because of their important role in Chinese cooking (but they are rather expensive). They should be soaked in warm water for 30 minutes or more, and sliced before use. The water in which they have been soaked may be used as stock. Their flavour is strong and distinctive — not at all like our cultivated (and somewhat tasteless) mushrooms, so only a few are needed to impart this flavour. There are other dried and tinned fungi available and, if you are adventurous, you should try them.

Noodles — these may be obtained dry in packets or fresh. There are many varieties of shape and they are made from several different ingredients. I prefer egg noodles which are made with wheat flour, but vegans can use rice vermicelli. To use noodles in chow mein or crispy noodles you need only soak them for 10 minutes in boiling water.

Sesame Oil — this is an expensive and highly nutritious oil which is rarely used for frying. It is more often added to dishes as a flavouring just before serving. Tahini, which is made from sesame seeds, and which is also called sesame jam by the Chinese, is also used in Chinese cookery.

Soya Sauce — this legendary ingredient of most Chinese dishes is available in bottles or cans. It is used liberally when cooking vegetables or noodles, as well as in sauces. Its saltiness means that salt is a rare ingredient in Chinese recipes.

SUGGESTED MENUS
for 6 people

Menu I	**Menu II**

Starters

| Pancake Rolls | Pancake Rolls |
| Sweet-Sour Sauce | Sweet-Sour Sauce |

Main Courses

Chow Mein	Fried Rice
Ratatouille Sauce	Stir-fried Vegetables
Stir-fried Vegetables	Peanut Butter Sauce
Chestnuts and Red Beans	Fried Tofu
	Crispy Noodles

Desserts

| Chinese Fruit Salad | Chinese Fruit Salad |

A. Starters

PANCAKE ROLLS

Imperial (Metric)	American
½ packet frozen pancake wrappers	½ packet frozen pancake wrappers
12 dried mushrooms	12 dried mushrooms
½ lb (¼ kilo) beansprouts	4 cupsful beansprouts
½ lb (¼ kilo) potatoes	½ pound potatoes
10 water chestnuts	10 water chestnuts
½ lb (¼ kilo) fresh tofu	1⅔ cupsful fresh tofu
2 tablespoonsful sesame oil	2 tablespoonsful sesame oil
2 tablespoonsful soya sauce	2 tablespoonsful soya sauce
Vegetable oil for deep frying	Vegetable oil for deep frying

1. Leave the pancake wrappers to thaw for 2 hours.

2. Soak the dried mushrooms for an hour and slice thinly.

3. Fry the beansprouts for a couple of minutes until tender.

4. Peel the potatoes and cook them until soft. Then drain and mash.

5. Chop the water chestnuts finely.

6. Stir-fry the mushrooms for a couple of minutes until they are tender.

7. Mix all the ingredients for the filling except the beansprouts.

8. Peel the pancake wrappers carefully one by one as required (they quickly dry up).

9. Place a tablespoonful of the filling diagonally and off-centre on the wrapper with ½ tablespoonful of beansprouts alongside. Fold over the corner, then roll the wrapper over the filling. Tuck in the corners and roll up tightly.

10. Without much delay (because the filling will soak through the wrapper) place the pancake roll in hot oil and fry until golden. You must take care that the pancake roll does not unwrap when it is in the oil.

11. Serve as soon as possible, either as a starter or dredged in sweet-sour sauce. If the pancake rolls are cooked too early, they will lose their crispness.

Note: Deep-frozen pancake wrappers can be obtained in packets of about 24 in most Chinese food shops.

SWEET-SOUR SAUCE

Imperial (Metric)	American
2 tablespoonsful sesame oil	2 tablespoonsful sesame oil
2 thin slices ginger, finely chopped	2 thin slices ginger, finely chopped
1 large carrot, thinly sliced	1 large carrot, thinly sliced
4 tablespoonsful tomato *purée*	4 tablespoonsful tomato paste
4 tablespoonsful sherry	4 tablespoonsful sherry
4 tablespoonsful cider vinegar	4 tablespoonsful cider vinegar
1 tablespoonful soya sauce	1 tablespoonful soya sauce
½ pint (¼ litre) stock (from the soaked mushrooms)	⅔ cupful stock (from the soaked mushrooms)
4 tablespoonsful arrowroot	4 tablespoonsful arrowroot
1 large red pepper, finely shredded	1 large red pepper, finely shredded
1 tablespoonful lemon juice	1 tablespoonful lemon juice
Raw cane sugar to taste	Raw cane sugar to taste

1. Heat the oil and fry the ginger and carrots over a low heat for 10 minutes.

2. Add the tomato *purée*, sherry, vinegar, soya sauce and stock.

3. Bring the sauce to the boil and, meanwhile, with a couple of tablespoonsful of liquid drawn from the sauce, mix the arrowroot to a paste in a bowl.

4. Add the arrowroot to the sauce and simmer for 10 minutes.

5. Add the shredded pepper and the lemon juice.

6. Test for sweetness and, if necessary, add sugar as required.

B. Main Courses

CHOW MEIN

Imperial (Metric)
1 lb (½ kilo) noodles
Vegetable oil for frying
1 medium onion, finely chopped
2 cloves garlic, crushed
½ lb (¼ kilo) white cabbage,
  shredded
1 tin bamboo shoot strip, drained
4 tablespoonsful soya sauce
20 dried mushrooms, soaked for at
  least 30 minutes
2 tablespoonsful hoisin sauce
4 tablespoonsful sherry
Ratatouille sauce (page 120)

American
3 cupsful noodles
Vegetable oil for frying
1 medium onion, finely chopped
2 cloves garlic, crushed
½ pound white cabbage, shredded
1 can bamboo shoot strip, drained
4 tablespoonsful soya sauce
20 dried mushrooms, soaked for at
  least 30 minutes
2 tablespoonsful hoisin sauce
4 tablespoonsful sherry
Ratatouille sauce (page 120)

1. Place the noodles in boiling water to cover and soak for 10 minutes.

2. Heat about 3 tablespoonsful of oil in a wok over a medium heat.

3. Add the onion and garlic and stir-fry until transparent.

4. Add the cabbage and bamboo shoots, stirring constantly for a
   further 3 minutes.

5. Add the drained noodles and 2 tablespoonsful of soya sauce and
   mix well. Stir on a medium heat for 3 or 4 minutes. The cabbage
   should still be crunchy.

6. Spread the noodles on a hot serving dish and keep hot in the oven.

7. Heat a little oil in the wok over a medium heat.

8. Slice the mushrooms and fry them for 1 minute.

9. Add 2 tablespoonsful of soya sauce, the hoisin sauce and sherry.
   Cook for 2 minutes.

10. Pour the mushrooms over the centre of the noodles and the Ratatouille Sauce around the mushrooms.

11. Return the dish to the oven and keep warm.

RATATOUILLE SAUCE

Imperial (Metric)	American
Vegetable oil for frying	Vegetable oil for frying
2 tablespoonsful salted black beans (dried or tinned)	2 tablespoonsful salted black beans (dried or tinned)
2 medium onions, finely chopped	2 medium onions, finely chopped
2 cloves garlic, crushed	2 cloves garlic, crushed
2 slices root ginger, finely chopped	2 slices root ginger, finely chopped
1 red pepper, chopped	1 red pepper, chopped
14 oz (400g) tin tomatoes	1 medium can tomatoes
1 medium aubergine, cubed	1 medium eggplant, cubed
2 courgettes, sliced	2 zucchini, sliced
1 tablespoonful hoisin sauce	1 tablespoonful hoisin sauce
Vegetable stock	Vegetable stock
4 tablespoonsful soya sauce	4 tablespoonsful soya sauce
3 tablespoonsful sesame oil (optional)	3 tablespoonsful sesame oil (optional)

1. Heat the oil in a wok and add the beans, onion, garlic, ginger and red pepper.

2. Stir-fry for 5 minutes over a medium heat. Do not allow this to burn.

3. Add the tomatoes, aubergine (eggplant) cubes, courgettes (zucchini) and hoisin sauce. Fry for a further 5 minutes.

4. Add about ½ cupful of vegetable stock and simmer for about 20 minutes.

5. Add more stock if necessary (or use some red wine) along with the soya sauce.

6. Stir and simmer for a further 20 minutes or until the liquid begins to thicken.

7. Add the sesame oil, if used, before spooning the sauce over the Chow Mein.

Note: The amount of sauce that you will require to dress the Chow Mein will depend on the surface area of the Chow Mein but if there is some sauce left over, it can be served as a side dish or stored in the refrigerator or freezer for a future occasion.

STIR-FRIED VEGETABLES

Imperial (Metric)	American
2 medium carrots	2 medium carrots
2 peppers (red and green, if available)	2 peppers (red and green, if available)
12 dried mushrooms, soaked for at least 30 minutes	12 dried mushrooms, soaked for at least 30 minutes
4 sticks celery	4 stalks celery
2 cloves garlic, crushed	2 cloves garlic, crushed
1 medium onion, finely chopped	1 medium onion, finely chopped
4 slices ginger, finely chopped	4 slices ginger, finely chopped
1 tin bamboo shoot strip, drained	1 can bamboo shoot strip, drained
1 lb (½ kilo) beansprouts, washed	1 pound beansprouts, washed
2 tablespoonsful sherry	2 tablespoonsful sherry
3 tablespoonsful soya sauce	3 tablespoonsful soya sauce
2 tablespoonsful sesame oil	2 tablespoonsful sesame oil

1. Cut the carrots, peppers and mushrooms into matchstick size pieces.

2. Slice the celery diagonally into 1 in. (2cm) segments.

3. Heat the oil in a wok. Stir-fry the garlic, onion and ginger for 2 minutes.

4. Add the mushrooms, carrots, drained bamboo shoots, celery and peppers. Finally add the beansprouts.

5. After a minute or so, add the sherry and soya sauce. Cook over a high flame for 2 or 3 minutes.

6. Just before serving add the sesame oil.

Note: Other vegetables which are excellent in this dish are baby sweetcorns (available tinned in Chinese shops), cauliflower, broccoli, water chestnuts and asparagus.

CHESTNUTS AND RED BEANS

Imperial (Metric)

4 tablespoonsful vegetable oil
2 slices root ginger, finely chopped
2 cloves garlic, crushed
½ lb (¼ kilo) dried red kidney
   beans, soaked and parboiled
½ lb (¼ kilo) dried chestnuts,
   soaked and parboiled
2 tablespoonsful soya sauce
Vegetable stock
Red wine
2 tablespoonsful sesame oil

American

4 tablespoonsful vegetable oil
2 slices root ginger, finely chopped
2 cloves garlic, crushed
1¼ cupsful dried red kidney beans,
   soaked and parboiled
½ pound dried chestnuts, soaked
   and parboiled
2 tablespoonsful soya sauce
Vegetable stock
Red wine
2 tablespoonsful sesame oil

1. Heat the oil in a wok and stir-fry the ginger and garlic for 2 minutes.

2. Add the red beans, chestnuts and other ingredients. Use enough red wine and stock to cover the beans and chestnuts.

3. Either cook on top of the stove or in the oven until the chestnuts and red beans are tender but not soft (this will depend on how long they have been parboiled).

SPICY PEANUT BUTTER SAUCE

Imperial (Metric)	American
½ lb (¼ kilo) peanut butter (preferably crunchy)	2 cupsful peanut butter (preferably crunchy)
4 tablespoonsful sesame oil	4 tablespoonsful sesame oil
4 tablespoonsful soya sauce	4 tablespoonsful soya sauce
4 tablespoonsful sherry	4 tablespoonsful sherry
2 tablespoonsful hoisin sauce	2 tablespoonsful hoisin sauce
2 tablespoonsful chilli sauce (or more, according to taste)	2 tablespoonsful chilli sauce (or more, according to taste)
Water or vegetable stock	Water or vegetable stock

1. Mix the ingredients over a low flame until smooth.

2. Add the stock or water if the sauce begins to thicken too much.

FRIED RICE

Imperial (Metric)	American
20 lily buds	20 lily buds
4 tablespoonsful vegetable oil	4 tablespoonsful vegetable oil
1 medium onion, finely chopped	1 medium onion, finely chopped
1 tin braised bamboo shoots	1 can braised bamboo shoots
4 oz (100g) button mushrooms, halved	2 cupsful button mushrooms, halved
2 oz (50g) cashew nuts	$\frac{1}{2}$ cupful cashew nuts
4 oz (100g) peas	$\frac{2}{3}$ cupful peas
4 oz (100g) sweetcorn	$\frac{2}{3}$ cupful sweetcorn
1 lb ($\frac{1}{2}$ kilo) cooked long-grain brown rice	2 cupsful cooked long-grain brown rice
3 tablespoonsful soya sauce	3 tablespoonsful soya sauce

1. Soak the lily buds for 30 minutes and drain.

2. Heat the oil in a wok and stir-fry the onion for 1 minute.

3. Add the drained lily buds, bamboo shoots, mushrooms and cashews.

4. Add the peas and sweetcorn.

5. Heat the rice in a large saucepan and pour in the contents of the wok; mix well.

6. Sprinkle the soya sauce over the rice.

FRIED TOFU

Imperial (Metric)	American
20 dried mushrooms	20 dried mushrooms
20 lily buds	20 lily buds
1½ lb (¾ kilo) fresh tofu	4 cupsful fresh tofu
Vegetable oil for deep-frying	Vegetable oil for deep-frying
½ tin bamboo shoot strip, drained	½ can bamboo shoot strip, drained
4 oz (100g) sultanas	⅔ cupful golden seedless raisins
2 tablespoonsful soya sauce	2 tablespoonsful soya sauce
1 tablespoonful arrowroot mixed with 1 tablespoonful water	1 tablespoonful arrowroot mixed with 1 tablespoonful water

1. Soak the mushrooms and lily buds for an hour.

2. Cut the tofu across the cubes into about 6 slices.

3. Deep-fry the tofu in the oil until it turns brown. About 6 chunks can be cooked simultaneously. They should float to the surface fairly quickly after being placed in the oil if it is hot enough. Avoid letting the tofu stick to the base of the pan.

4. Drain the tofu and keep warm.

5. Cut the mushrooms into thin strips and stir-fry with the lily buds and bamboo shoots. Add the sultanas (golden seedless raisins) and soya sauce and continue to stir-fry for 5 minutes.

6. Add the arrowroot and allow to thicken. Then pour the mixture over the fried tofu.

CRISPY NOODLES

Imperial (Metric)
1 lb (½ kilo) egg noodles
Vegetable oil for deep frying

American
1 pound egg noodles
Vegetable oil for deep frying

1. Immerse the noodles in boiling water for 10 minutes.

2. Place on a damp tea-cloth to drain.

3. Heat the oil and fry handfuls of the drained noodles until crisp. This will take 15 to 20 seconds if the oil is hot.

4. Serve topped with Ratatouille Sauce (page 120) or plain with a sprinkling of soya sauce.

C. Dessert

CHINESE FRUIT SALAD

Imperial (Metric)
1 medium melon
2 large oranges
3 kiwi fruits
1 tin lychees
1 tablespoonful toasted sesame
　seeds

American
1 medium melon
2 large oranges
3 kiwi fruits
1 can lychees
1 tablespoonful toasted sesame
　seeds

1. Cube the melon. Peel the orange and discard as much pith and skin as possible. Halve each segment.

2. Rub the kiwi fruit (also known as Chinese gooseberry) until it is free of 'hairs' and then slice.

3. Combine the melon and orange pieces with the kiwi fruit slices and mix with the lychees and the juice from the tin.

4. Serve in glasses topped with toasted sesame seeds.

D. Drink

CHINESE PUNCH

Imperial (Metric)	American
1 tin lychees	1 can lychees
1 lb (½ kilo) fresh cumquats	1 pound fresh cumquats
½ bottle vodka	½ bottle vodka
1 bottle dry white wine	1 bottle dry white wine
4 drops Angostura bitters	4 drops Angostura bitters
½ pint (¼ litre) orange juice	1¾ cupsful orange juice

1. Drain the lychees, reserving the liquid.

2. Halve the cumquats (or pit and halve the cherries).

3. Soak the prepared fruit in the vodka for about 3 hours.

4. Throw in the wine, Angostura bitters and juices and sample.

Note: If cumquats are unobtainable, cherries or pineapple are also excellent in this punch.

8.

EASTERN EUROPE

Each of the Eastern European countries contributes at least one dish to this meal. Of course, the region is a vast one and the type of food consumed varies greatly from the east to the west. One feature, perhaps, is the use of sour cream or yogurt in several dishes of the area; another is the use of tasty fresh vegetables such as peppers, beetroot and mushrooms.

Some vegetarians have an objection to using textured vegetable protein (tvp) because they feel that they should not crave anything that tastes like meat and that tvp is a processed food. There are many counters to these arguments and I believe that if these people tasted a well-cooked meatless stroganoff or goulash they would soon change their opinion. Stroganoff is a rich, creamy dish in which the tvp is cooked in sour cream with the additional flavouring of onions, garlic, mushrooms, and mustard. The fiery redness of the Goulash gives it 'eye appeal', but its aroma and flavour, originating mostly from the red peppers, are as good as its appearance.

Potato dishes abound in Eastern European countries and it is interesting to notice similarities between the potato pancakes of Czechoslovakia or Poland and those of Ireland. The Czechoslovakian Potato Cake chosen here is excellent but I have had to adapt the cooking method so that a sufficient quantity can be produced in a shortish spell of time. An effective non-stick pan will greatly help you in the preparation of this dish as will be evident from the recipe. The cake will be built up in layers (I have suggested three cakes can be made from the quantities given) and when they are together on one plate you may decide that its appearance is improved by grilling it until evenly brown. Alternatively, you may prefer to serve the cakes separately.

Rumania contributes a beautifully creamy dish of mushrooms in a sour cream sauce which, when served, is similar in appearance to the Stroganoff, so that if one dish were to be omitted from this array, it should be one of these two dishes. The quantity of mushrooms may seem excessive but they cook down in volume considerably. Dill, the most widely used herb in this area, gives this dish a flavour which distinguishes it from the Stroganoff.

Rumania's neighbour, Bulgaria, gives us Bajaldo, a time-consuming dish to prepare, and best made with small aubergines (eggplants) so that they are evenly roasted. The strong aroma and beautiful taste of the aubergines (eggplants) and white wine will make the effort expended in the preparation of the dish seem worth while.

Several excellent Polish vegetarian dishes exist as this country has a much richer cuisine than many of her neighbours. Edible fungi, noodles, sauerkraut and a range of tasty potato dishes are among excellent vegetarian dishes from this mainly agricultural country. I have chosen a beetroot dish as, unless Bortsch is served as a first course, it would be a crime to omit this delicious and colourful vegetable from the meal, particularly as this way of cooking it is sadly overlooked in this country.

The black peasant bread should not be despised for any reason, least of all because it is the fare of some of the poorest people in the world. Indeed, the aristocrats who returned to the countryside in the summers continued to enjoy the traditional peasant foods. This bread is ideal to accompany the Aubergine and Pepper 'Caviare' from Yugoslavia, a dish which reflects the hot sunny summers which the country enjoys and which make it such a popular tourist area.

A dish is usually described as Hungarian if it is cooked with the addition of paprika. While the dish I have suggested traditionally uses courgettes (zucchini), I find that pumpkin is at least as good. Try cooking both courgettes (zucchini) and pumpkin in this way and decide where your own preference lies.

For a dessert, try the Russian Cream which is a rich, sweet, delicately flavoured dish, or the Poppy-seed Torte from Germany. Black poppy seeds are used in many Eastern European desserts and have an unusual but pleasant texture and flavour.

There are some excellent wines of this vast area, especially in Yugoslavia (Reisling) and Bulgaria (Chardonnay). However, the major alcoholic drink in the larger part of this area is Vodka. I can recommend cherry Vodka from Poland and lemon Vodka from Leningrad, which are both pleasant and unusual drinks. Slivovitz, or plum brandy, is a famous spirit of Bulgaria, and Czechoslovakia produces *Pils* lager which is found even in this country.

SUGGESTED MENUS
for 6 people

Menu I   Menu II

Starters

Black Bread   Black Bread
Aubergine and Pepper Pâté   Aubergine and Pepper Pâté

Main Courses

Stroganoff   Goulash
Czechoslovakian Potato Cake   Mushrooms in Sour Cream
Polish Beetroot Purée   Hungarian Pumpkin
Bajaldo   Polish Beetroot Purée

Desserts

Russian Cream   Poppy-seed Torte

RECIPES
A. Starters

BLACK PEASANT BREAD
Russia

Imperial (Metric)	American
¾ pint (400ml) hot water	2 cupsful hot water
4 tablespoonsful molasses	4 tablespoonsful molasses
¾ oz (20g) dried yeast	1½ tablespoonsful dried yeast
¼ pint (150ml) warm water	⅔ cupful warm water
1 teaspoonful raw cane sugar	1 teaspoonful raw cane sugar
1½ lb (¾ kilo) rye flour	6 cupsful rye flour
1 teaspoonful sea salt	1 teaspoonful sea salt
3 tablespoonsful vegetable oil	3 tablespoonsful vegetable oil

1. Put the hot water into a bowl and add the molasses. Mix well.

2. Dissolve the yeast in the warm water and add the sugar. Let it stand in a warm place for about 15 minutes.

3. Stir the yeast and molasses into the rye flour and add the salt and oil.

4. Put the dough into a greased bowl and cover. Leave in a warm place for about 15 minutes.

5. Knead the dough for about 10 minutes.

6. Put the dough back into the greased bowl and leave in a warm place for about 90 minutes until double the original size.

7. Form into one large loaf or two smaller loaves. Make the loaves as high as possible as they will spread out and flatten while baking.

8. Place on a piece of greaseproof paper and allow to rise for 30 minutes.

9. Bake for 40 minutes at 400°F/200°C (Gas Mark 6).

Note: Rye flour is rather sticky and you may prefer to use some wholemeal flour instead of the rye, perhaps using half of each.

AUBERGINE AND PEPPER PÂTÉ
Yugoslavia

Imperial (Metric)	American
3 medium aubergines	3 medium eggplants
3 peppers, preferably red	3 peppers, preferably red
3 cloves garlic, crushed	3 cloves garlic, crushed
Up to 6 tablespoonsful olive oil	Up to 6 tablespoonsful olive oil
Sea salt and pepper	Sea salt and pepper
2 tablespoonsful lemon juice	2 tablespoonsful lemon juice
2 tablespoonsful peanut butter or tahini	2 tablespoonsful peanut butter or tahini

1. Put the aubergines (eggplants) and peppers into a very hot oven at 450°F/230°C (Gas Mark 8) and cook until they are tender and the skin is blackening.

2. Skin them as best as you can and blend well with all the other ingredients except the peanut butter or tahini.

3. Stir in the peanut butter or tahini until you have the desired consistency.

Note: Either tahini or peanut butter may be used to thicken this dish, which, along with hummus, is a vegetarian pâté to rival any meat pâté.

B. Main Courses

STROGANOFF
Russia

Imperial (Metric)	American
½ lb (¼ kilo) tvp, rehydrated in white wine	2 cupsful tvp, rehydrated in white wine
4 medium onions, finely chopped	4 medium onions, finely chopped
3 cloves garlic, crushed	3 cloves garlic, crushed
3 oz (75g) butter	⅓ cupful butter
½ lb (¼ kilo) mushrooms, sliced	3 cupsful mushrooms, sliced
½ pint (¼ litre) sour cream	⅔ cupful sour cream
Sea salt and pepper	Sea salt and pepper
1 teaspoonful mild French mustard	1 teaspoonful mild French mustard

1. Strain off the excess liquid from the tvp, and reserve it.

2. Fry the onions and garlic in the butter for a few minutes.

3. Add the tvp and mushrooms. Stir and continue to cook over a medium heat for 5 minutes or so.

4. Add the sour cream, salt, freshly ground black pepper and mustard.

5. Simmer gently until the tvp is tender. Add the reserved liquid if necessary.

GOULASH
Hungary

Imperial (Metric)	**American**
½ lb (¼ kilo) tvp, rehydrated in red wine	2 cupsful tvp, rehydrated in red wine
4 oz (100g) butter	½ cupful butter
6 cloves garlic, crushed	6 cloves garlic, crushed
6 medium onions, thinly sliced	6 medium onions, thinly sliced
8 tinned red peppers, roughly chopped	8 canned red peppers, roughly chopped
2 14 oz (400g) tins tomatoes	2 medium cans tomatoes
2 tablespoonsful tomato *purée*	2 tablespoonsful tomato paste
Sea salt	Sea salt
2 teaspoonsful paprika	2 teaspoonsful paprika

1. Drain off the tvp and reserve any excess liquid.

2. Melt half the butter and fry the tvp and garlic for about 10 minutes.

3. Fry the onions in the rest of the butter until they become transparent.

4. Add the peppers, tomatoes, reserved liquid and tomato *purée* to the onions and season with the sea salt and paprika.

5. Add the tvp and cook gently for about 40 minutes or until the tvp is tender.

Note: If fresh red peppers are used, they should be roasted and peeled before being added to this dish. Carrots and new potatoes could be included if the full range of dishes of the dinner party is not being prepared. The flavour can be varied by the use of marjoram or caraway seeds. Rehydrating the tvp in beer would be a further interesting variation.

BRAMBOROVY GULAS (POTATO CAKE)
Czechoslovakia

Imperial (Metric)
2 medium onions, finely chopped
¼ pint (150ml) vegetable oil (olive
  oil is best)
3 lb (1½ kilo) potatoes, peeled and
  finely diced
2 teaspoonsful paprika
Seasoning
3 bay leaves
½ pint (¼ litre) yogurt
3 oz (75g) wholemeal flour
4 tablespoonsful parsley

American
2 medium onions, finely chopped
⅔ cupful vegetable oil (olive oil is
  best)
3 pounds potatoes, peeled and finely
  diced
2 teaspoonsful paprika
Seasoning
3 bay leaves
1⅓ cupsful yogurt
¾ cupful wholewheat flour
4 tablespoonsful parsley

1. In a large non-stick pan fry the onions in some of the oil until they become transparent.

2. Add the potatoes together with the paprika, salt, freshly ground black pepper and bay leaves.

3. Cover the pan and cook gently until the potatoes are just tender.

4. Mix the yogurt and flour and add to the potatoes.

5. Take a third or quarter of the mixture and put it into a frying pan with some oil. Increase the heat to brown the potato cake.

6. Turn the potato cake onto a large plate and keep it warm under a grill or in the oven while you make the other cakes.

7. Pile the potato cakes up on the large plate and brown the top evenly under the grill.

8. Garnish with parsley before serving.

Note: Many variations of this recipe are possible, but to facilitate the cooking of the cakes, it is best to put all the diced potatoes in a large pan with the onions to cook gently for 15 to 20 minutes. Three or four cakes can then be made in a smaller frying pan.

CIUIAMA DE CIUPERCI (Mushrooms in Sour Cream)
Rumania

Most countries of Eastern Europe have a mushroom dish as one of their national delicacies. There is nothing to compare with the flavour of the *cep* which is found commonly in France (*les cèpes*), Italy (*porcini*), in Eastern Europe and in this country. Even cultivated mushrooms are excellent in this dish.

Imperial (Metric)	American
2 medium onions, finely chopped	2 medium onions, finely chopped
3 oz (75g) butter	1/3 cupful butter
2 lb (1 kilo) mushrooms	2 pounds mushrooms
Seasoning	Seasoning
2 tablespoonsful wholemeal flour	2 tablespoonsful wholewheat flour
1/2 pint (1/4 litre) sour cream	1 1/3 cupsful sour cream
1/2 teaspoonful dill	1/2 teaspoonful dill
Parsley to garnish	Parsley to garnish

1. Fry the onions in the butter until transparent.

2. Add the mushrooms (leave button mushrooms whole and halve larger ones).

3. Add salt and freshly ground black pepper and cook gently for about 15 minutes.

4. Stir in the flour and add the sour cream gradually, followed by the dill.

5. Heat gently until the mushrooms are cooked.

6. Garnish with parsley.

BAJALDO (Aubergines Cooked in White Wine)
Bulgaria

Imperial (Metric)	American
6 medium aubergines	6 medium eggplants
Sea salt	Sea salt
Lemon juice	Lemon juice
4 oz (100g) wholemeal flour	1 cupful wholewheat flour
¼ pint (150ml) olive oil	⅔ cupful olive oil
3 medium onions, finely chopped	3 medium onions, finely chopped
6 tablespoonsful parsley	6 tablespoonsful parsley
½ bottle white wine	½ bottle white wine

1. Put the aubergines (eggplants) on a spit under a high heat for about 10 minutes.

2. Peel them and cut into slices about ½ in. (1cm) thick.

3. Add salt and pour lemon juice over the aubergine (eggplant) slices. Let them stand for 30 minutes then drain and rinse.

4. Coat the slices with flour.

5. Heat the oil and fry the slices on both sides.

6. Put the aubergine (eggplant) slices into a casserole dish.

7. Chop the onions and parsley and sprinkle over the aubergine (eggplant).

8. Add the wine and place the dish in the oven.

9. Bake in a moderate oven at 350°F/180°C (Gas Mark 4) until all the wine has evaporated or soaked into the aubergines (eggplants).

BEETROOT PURÉE
Poland

Imperial (Metric)	American
1 lb (½ kilo) cooking apples	1 pound cooking apples
2 lb (1 kilo) raw beetroot	2 pounds raw beet
2 medium onions, finely chopped	2 medium onions, finely chopped
4 tablespoonsful vegetable oil	4 tablespoonsful vegetable oil
Seasoning	Seasoning
2 tablespoonsful lemon juice	2 tablespoonsful lemon juice
2 tablespoonsful horseradish, grated	2 tablespoonsful horseradish, grated
½ pint (¼ litre) sour cream	1⅓ cupsful sour cream
2 oz (50g) wholemeal flour	½ cupful wholewheat flour

1. Peel the apples and beetroot (beet) and grate coarsely.

2. Fry the onions in the oil for 2 minutes.

3. Add the beetroot (beet) and apples and any juice that has come from them.

4. Season well and add the lemon juice and horseradish.

5. Simmer, covered, for 30 minutes.

6. Add half the sour cream and the flour and cook for a further 15 minutes.

7. Stir the remainder of the sour cream into the beetroot (beet) *purée* just before serving to give an attractive streaky effect.

HUNGARIAN PUMPKIN

Imperial (Metric)	American
2 lb (900g) pumpkin or marrow	2 pounds pumpkin or summer squash
6 oz (150g) butter	¾ cupful butter
2 teaspoonsful paprika	2 teaspoonsful paprika
4 medium onions, finely chopped	4 medium onions, finely chopped
¼ pint (150ml) wine vinegar	⅔ cupful wine vinegar
1 tablespoonful dill seeds	1 tablespoonful dill seeds
2 teaspoonsful raw cane sugar	2 teaspoonsful raw cane sugar

1. Peel the pumpkin, discarding the seeds. Dice into about ½ in. (1cm) cubes.

2. Melt 4 oz (100g/½ cupful) of butter in a large pan. Add the pumpkin and fry quickly for 4 minutes. Shake the pan to prevent sticking.

3. Add the paprika.

4. Meanwhile fry the onions with the rest of the butter.

5. Cover for 3 minutes and then add the vinegar, dill and sugar.

6. Add the onions to the pumpkin and simmer for 5 minutes, by which time it should be just tender.

C. Desserts

RUSSIAN CREAM

Imperial (Metric)	American
1 lb (½ kilo) curd cheese	2 cupsful curd cheese
2 oz (50g) Demerara sugar, ground	⅓ cupful Demerara sugar, ground
2 oz (50g) almonds, blanched and slivered	½ cupful almonds, blanched and slivered
2 oz (50g) raisins	⅓ cupful raisins
2 oz (50g) dried apricots, halved	2 ounces dried apricots, halved
2 tablespoonsful lemon juice	2 tablespoonsful lemon juice
1 teaspoonful vanilla essence	1 teaspoonful vanilla essence
2 teaspoonsful preserved ginger, chopped	2 teaspoonsful preserved ginger, chopped
½ pint (¼ litre) double cream, whipped	1⅓ cupsful heavy cream, whipped

1. Mix all the ingredients except the double cream together and put into a pudding basin. Leave overnight to set.

2. Turn out onto a dish or serve in individual glass dishes topped with double (heavy) cream.

POPPY-SEED TORTE

Imperial (Metric)	American
4 oz (100g) black poppy seeds	¾ cupful black poppy seeds
3 oz (75g) raisins	½ cupful raisins
½ teaspoonful cloves, ground	½ teaspoonful cloves, ground
4 tablespoonsful rum (or more)	4 tablespoonsful rum (or more)
Rind from ½ lemon, grated	Rind from ½ lemon, grated
1 teaspoonful cinnamon	1 teaspoonful cinnamon
10 eggs, separated	10 eggs, separated
½ lb (¼ kilo) Demerara sugar	1⅓ cupsful Demerara sugar
1 pint (½ litre) double cream, whipped	2½ cupsful heavy cream, whipped

1. Soak the raisins in the rum overnight and then drain well.

2. Grind the poppy seeds as finely as possible.

3. Beat the sugar with the egg yolks until creamy.

4. Add the raisins, cinnamon, cloves, lemon rind and poppy seeds and mix well.

5. Fold in the egg whites beaten to a light froth.

6. Place greaseproof paper on two 9 in. (23cm) cake tins and pour half of the mixture in each.

7. Bake in an oven preset to 350°F/180°C (Gas Mark 4) for about an hour.

8. Remove from the tins and allow to cool.

9. Brush the torte halves with rum on one side each and place these rummed sides together with half of the whipped cream between them.

10. Pipe the whipped cream on top of the torte and serve.

9.

CELTIC FOOD

Although they are prominent, there is more to this menu than oatmeal, leeks and potatoes. It would be true to say that if you were aiming to impress non-vegetarians with exotic and expensive food, you would not choose this dinner party, but as a warming conclusion to a cold day, and as an example of economy cooking, vegetarian style, this is an excellent meal. Not that it is uninteresting — the Tipperary Pie, for example, is a tasty combination of tvp and root vegetables, baked in a pastry crust so that the full flavour of the filling is developed.

An obvious starter is Welsh Rarebit, which is rather more than just cheese on toast. Stout, strong ale or cider can be used to make the cheese mixture and this suggests the most appropriate accompanying drink. Alternatively, Colcannon is a tasty dish which would stand on its own as a starter dish. Colcannon is little more than an Irish form of 'bubble-and-squeak', and it can be varied by the omission of cheese, the use of curly kale instead of cabbage, or by using milk or chives. Traditionally, the whole frying pan is used to make one large 'cake' of Colcannon, but smaller 'cakes' are easier to cook and serve.

You should choose between the Leek Pie and Tipperary Pie as both of these have a high proportion of pastry. Both are hearty dishes with their traditions in the rugged country of the Welsh or Irish rural areas.

The main Scottish contributions to the meal are cheap yet substantial dishes. The Oatmeal and Carrot Pudding is simple to prepare and it combines well with the Brown Sauce to make a cheering winter dish. Scotch Eggs with vegetarian ingredients are most tasty but they are time-consuming to prepare. They can be made well in advance, however.

Pan-kail is an interesting way of serving any greens, but frozen spinach is particularly suitable and this is a delicious way of serving the vegetable. Swede Purry is also a good way of serving a much under-rated vegetable, though turnips or even parsnips could be used just as well.

There are many Irish recipes using potatoes: Champ, Stelk, Murphies, Fadge and Boxty pancakes. The latter are excellent on their own as a snack and could be combined with Welsh Rarebit as part of the starter.

While traditional drinks are whisky, Guinness and mead, unless you can make your own mead so that you can have a fairly dry drink to accompany the meal, I would recommend a rosé, sparkling wine or cider.

It would be unreasonable to exclude whisky altogether, and the Scottish Posset is a perfect light dessert at the end of the meal. As an alternative, you could serve oatcakes with Caerphilly and Orkney cheeses, accompanied, of course, with a wee dram.

SUGGESTED MENUS
for 6 people

Menu I	**Menu II**

Starters

Colcannon	Welsh Rarebit

Main Courses

Welsh Leek Pie	Tipperary Pie
Oatmeal and Carrot Pudding	Scotch Eggs
Brown Sauce	Brown Sauce
Swede Purry	Pan-Kail
Pan-Kail	Boxty Pancakes

Desserts

Oatcakes	Scottish Posset
Scottish Cheeses	
Caerphilly	

A. Starters

WELSH RAREBIT
Wales

Imperial (Metric)	American
6 slices wholemeal bread, toasted on each side	6 slices wholewheat bread, toasted on each side
1 clove garlic	1 clove garlic
3 oz (75g) butter	⅓ cupful butter
2 oz (50g) wholemeal flour	½ cupful wholewheat flour
¼ pint (150ml) brown ale	⅔ cupful brown ale
6 oz (150g) Cheddar cheese, grated	1½ cupsful Cheddar cheese, grated
1 tablespoonful *Holbrook's* Worcestershire sauce	1 tablespoonful *Holbrook's* Worcestershire sauce
2 tablespoonsful cider vinegar	2 tablespoonsful cider vinegar
1 teaspoonful wholegrain mustard	1 teaspoonful wholegrain mustard
Freshly ground black pepper	Freshly ground black pepper
Sea salt	Sea salt
2 egg yolks	2 egg yolks

1. Rub the slices of toast with garlic and butter them.

2. Melt the remaining butter and add the flour. Cook slowly for a few minutes.

3. Stir in the ale slowly.

4. Stir in the Cheddar until thoroughly melted.

5. Add the Worcestershire sauce, cider vinegar, mustard and seasoning.

6. Lastly add the egg yolks and cook for a further 5 minutes, stirring constantly.

7. Cover each slice of toast with the rarebit and brown under the grill.

COLCANNON
Ireland

Imperial (Metric)	American
3 oz (75g) butter	⅓ cupful butter
1 medium onion, finely chopped	1 medium onion, finely chopped
½ cabbage, coarsely chopped	½ cabbage, coarsely chopped
1 lb (½ kilo) potatoes, mashed	1 pound potatoes, mashed
3 oz (75g) Cheddar cheese, grated	¾ cupful Cheddar cheese, grated

1. Melt a little butter in a frying pan and fry the onion until lightly browned.

2. Boil the cabbage until barely tender.

3. Mix the onion, potato and cabbage in a bowl and form the mixture into round cakes about 3 in. (7cm) in diameter and ½ in. (1cm) deep.

4. Melt the remaining butter in the frying pan and fry the cakes until partly brown on each side (they will not brown evenly).

5. Put a little Cheddar on each and place under a grill so that the cheese melts.

6. Serve hot, possibly garnished with parsley.

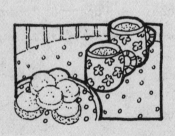

B. Main Courses

LEEK PIE
Wales

Imperial (Metric)
.4 oz (100g) butter
1 medium onion, sliced
1 lb (½ kilo) leeks, cleaned and
  sliced
¼ pint (150ml) single cream
1 tablespoonful wholemeal flour
Sea salt
Black pepper
1 lb (½ kilo) shortcrust pastry
  (page 88)
1 egg, beaten (to glaze)

American
½ cupful butter
1 medium onion, sliced
1 pound leeks, cleaned and sliced
⅔ cupful light cream
1 tablespoonful wholewheat flour
Sea salt
Black pepper
1 pound shortcrust pastry
  (page 88)
1 egg, beaten (to glaze)

1. Melt half the butter and fry the onion until transparent.

2. Add the leeks along with the rest of the butter and cook slowly
    for about 10 minutes.

3. Combine the cream and flour and stir this mixture into the
    vegetables.

4. Cook for a couple of minutes to thicken.

5. Season well with salt and pepper (or nutmeg, if you prefer).

6. Make a pie case with half the pastry and fill with the leek mixture.
    Cover with remaining pastry and seal well at the edges.

7. Glaze with beaten egg and make a hole in the centre to allow steam
    to escape.

8. Bake at 350°F/180°C (Gas Mark 4) for 45 minutes until the pastry
    is beginning to brown.

TIPPERARY PIE
Ireland

Imperial (Metric)	American
6 oz (150g) tvp, rehydrated in red wine or stock	1½ cupsful tvp, rehydrated in red wine or stock
1 leek, chopped	1 leek, chopped
2 carrots, diced	2 carrots, diced
½ swede, diced	½ swede, diced
1 parsnip, diced	1 parsnip, diced
Sea salt	Sea salt
Pepper	Pepper
1 teaspoonful mixed herbs	1 teaspoonful mixed herbs
3 tablespoonsful soya sauce	3 tablespoonsful soya sauce

For the Pastry:

Imperial (Metric)	American
½ lb (¼ kilo) wholemeal flour	2 cupsful wholewheat flour
2 oz (50g) vegetable margarine	5 tablespoonsful vegetable margarine
2 oz (50g) vegetable fat	5 tablespoonsful vegetable fat
1 teaspoonful sea salt	1 teaspoonful sea salt
1 teaspoonful baking powder	1 teaspoonful baking soda
Water	Water

1. Soak the tvp in wine or stock (or stout) for at least an hour.

2. Put it in a pan with the vegetables and seasonings.

3. Simmer for 30 minutes, adding further liquid if necessary.

4. Make the pastry by mixing the flour with the fat, salt and baking powder. Add enough water to make the pastry of the right consistency.

5. Roll out the pastry to fit a casserole. Fill with the tvp mixture and put a pastry lid on.

6. Bake at 350°F/180°C (Gas Mark 4) for 50 minutes.

Note: Any combination of root vegetables and other vegetables such as celery, onions or butter beans can be used — the only rule to keep is to ensure that at least 50 per cent, by volume, of the filling is vegetable. Flavourings could be varied: yeast extract, mustard, tomato *purée* or chilli sauce could be used, as could a variety of herbs.

OATMEAL AND CARROT PUDDING

Imperial (Metric)	American
1 lb (½ kilo) oatmeal	1 pound oatmeal
4 medium onions, finely chopped	4 medium onions, finely chopped
4 oz (100g) vegetable fat	½ cupful vegetable fat
1 lb (½ kilo) carrots, grated	1 pound carrots, grated
1 teaspoonful black pepper	1 teaspoonful black pepper
1 teaspoonful sea salt	1 teaspoonful sea salt

1. Bake the oatmeal in the oven at 350°F/180°C (Gas Mark 4) for 20 minutes until browning.

2. Cook the onions slowly in the vegetable fat until transparent.

3. Add the seasoning and carrots.

4. Stir in the oatmeal and mix well.

5. Put the mixture into a bowl, uncovered.

6. Place the bowl in a saucepan with water halfway up the sides and steam for 2 hours.

7. Serve with Brown Sauce (page 156).

PAN-KAIL
Scotland

Imperial (Metric)
2 lb (1 kilo) spinach *purée*
4 tablespoonsful oatmeal
Seasoning
1 pint (½ litre) single cream

American
2 pounds spinach *purée*
4 tablespoonsful oatmeal
Seasoning
2 cupsful light cream

1. Warm the spinach through and add the oatmeal.

2. Season well with sea salt and black pepper (a little nutmeg could also be added).

3. Just before serving, stir in the cream.

Note: Frozen spinach is used for convenience but any greens could be substituted if preferred.

BOXTY PANCAKES

Imperial (Metric)	American
½ lb (¼ kilo) potatoes, grated	½ pound potatoes, grated
½ lb (¼ kilo) potatoes, cooked and mashed	½ pound potatoes, cooked and mashed
4 oz (100g) wholemeal flour	1 cupful wholewheat flour
2 teaspoonsful sea salt	2 teaspoonsful sea salt
¼ pint (150ml) milk	⅔ cupful milk
2 eggs	2 eggs
Vegetable oil for frying	Vegetable oil for frying

1. Put the grated potato into a muslin bag and squeeze to get rid of as much moisture as possible.

2. Mix in the other ingredients to make a fairly stiff batter.

3. Leave to stand for 30 minutes.

4. Fry like pancakes in the oil until brown on each side. Serve hot.

Note: It is important for the success of this dish to squeeze excess moisture from the raw potatoes before mixing with the mashed potato.

SWEDE PURRY
Scotland

Imperial (Metric)	American
2 lb (1 kilo) swedes, diced	2 pounds rutabaga, diced
Seasoning	Seasoning
3 oz (75g) butter	⅓ cupful butter

1. Cook the swedes (rutabaga) until tender.

2. Mash the swedes (rutabaga) with the butter and season well.

3. Put the purry in a hot dish and keep hot until required.

SCOTCH EGGS

Imperial (Metric)	American
4 oz (100g) mashed potato	¾ cupful mashed potato
1 medium onion, grated	1 medium onion, grated
1 clove garlic, crushed	1 clove garlic, crushed
4 oz (100g) Brazil nuts, ground	¾ cupful Brazil nuts, ground
1 tablespoonful oil	1 tablespoonful oil
1 tablespoonful tomato *purée*	1 tablespoonful tomato paste
1 teaspoonful thyme	1 teaspoonful thyme
1 teaspoonful yeast extract	1 teaspoonful yeast extract
Black pepper	Black pepper
3 eggs, hard-boiled	3 eggs, hard-boiled
1 egg, beaten	1 egg, beaten
4 oz (100g) dry, fine breadcrumbs	1½ cupful dry, fine breadcrumbs
Oil for deep-frying	Oil for deep-frying

1. Mix the potato, onion, garlic, nuts, tomato *purée*, thyme, yeast extract and seasoning. Add liquid if required.

2. Coat the hard-boiled eggs with the nut mix as evenly as possible.

3. Dip each Scotch Egg in the beaten egg and breadcrumbs and fry in the hot oil until golden brown.

Note: While it seems more reasonable to use a nutmeat base in which to surround the hard-boiled eggs, you could use a mashed potato and cheese mixture. The nutmeat base used here can be varied widely by use of different sorts of nuts, and by varying the flavourings with *Holbrook's* Worcestershire sauce, mushrooms, herbs, leeks etc. Egg may be needed to bind the nutmix but should be avoided if possible.

BROWN SAUCE

Imperial (Metric)	American
2 tablespoonsful vegetable oil	2 tablespoonsful vegetable oil
1 medium onion, finely chopped	1 medium onion, finely chopped
3 tablespoonsful wholemeal flour	3 tablespoonsful wholewheat flour
2 pints (1 litre) vegetable stock	5 cupsful vegetable stock
2 bay leaves	2 bay leaves
2 teaspoonsful yeast extract	2 teaspoonsful yeast extract
3 tablespoonsful tomato *purée*	3 tablespoonsful tomato paste
Black pepper	Black pepper

1. Fry the onion in the oil until transparent.

2. Add the flour and stir for 5 minutes.

3. Add the liquid slowly, followed by the bay leaves and yeast extract.

4. Simmer for 10 minutes.

5. Extract the bay leaves, and put the sauce in a blender to make smooth.

6. Add the tomato *purée* and pepper (and salt, if required).

C. Dessert

SCOTTISH POSSET

Imperial (Metric)	American
2 lemons	2 lemons
3 eggs, separated	3 eggs, separated
3 tablespoonsful honey	3 tablespoonsful honey
4 tablespoonsful whisky	4 tablespoonsful whisky
½ pint (¼ litre) yogurt	1⅓ cupsful yogurt
½ pint (¼ litre) double cream, whipped	1⅓ cupsful heavy cream, whipped
2 oz (50g) oatmeal	½ cupful oatmeal

1. Grate the rind from the lemons and extract their juice.

2. Beat together the lemon rind, lemon juice, egg yolks, honey and whisky.

3. Whisk the egg white until it holds its shape.

4. Combine the yogurt, cream and egg white.

5. Use a spoon to stir in the lemon juice and whisky mixture.

6. Put into glasses and leave to chill and set.

7. Meanwhile, brown the oatmeal in the oven at 350°F/180°C (Gas Mark 4) for 20 minutes and allow to cool.

8. Sprinkle a little oatmeal over each glass just before serving.

10.
FESTIVE DINNER PARTY

Although this dinner party was devised for Christmas-time, it is equally suitable for any festive occasion such as other holiday times or birthdays.

The traditions of Christmas require the slaughter of several million turkeys and this is difficult to justify under any circumstances. It is impossible to justify if a delicious nutritious alternative is available, and, of course, there is. Many combinations of nuts, backings (such as mashed potato, rice or breadcrumbs), flavourings and binding are possible and these are the four constituents of a nut savoury. This can then be formed into burgers and baked, fried, or steamed in one dish. This can form the centre-piece of your festive meal, together with either a red wine sauce or a Brown Sauce (page 156).

I have not given a simple nut-roast here as I wish to show further variations on this theme: Chestnut Pie, Walnut Balls and Steamed Nutmeat. Chestnuts are a traditional Christmas food and the *purée* can be made from fresh chestnuts or bought in tins. The pie goes with the red wine sauce extremely well. Note that other nutmeat mixtures can be used in a pastry case and richer pastries can be used, if you wish.

The Walnut Balls can be served as a side dish with the Chestnut Pie, or as a main dish. In this case, I would serve them with a Béchamel Sauce.

The Steamed Nutmeat is a simple mixture of rich ingredients which is nourishing and tasty if rather heavy. It should be steamed for at least two hours, so, like the Christmas Pudding it can be prepared well in advance.

As a starter, I would serve a creamy, spicy Avocado Pâté with Crispbread, or Asparagus Quiche. These are both delicate, light starters which are particularly appropriate for this meal.

As vegetable accompaniments to the main course, there are the traditional vegetables such as sprouts (whole chestnuts combine well with them), parsnips, cauliflower and potatoes. As a variation to a fairly plain form, there are recipes included here which you will enjoy, such as Parsnips in Yogurt. However, roast parsnips are a favourite with most people so you could equally well serve these. Other ideas are peas with pecan nuts or braised celery.

Christmas Pudding is a dessert which should be served occasionally throughout the winter. It is a pity that some families eat it only at Christmas after a massive main course when it is less appreciated.

A recipe for mincemeat is given and with this you can make your own Mince Pies or an alternative dessert — the Mincemeat and Apple Crumble.

To drink with this meal, I would choose a dry white wine such as Macon Blanc, to be followed by a claret with the main course and port to sip with Mince Pies.

SUGGESTED MENUS
for 6 people

Menu I   **Menu II**

Starters

Avocado Pâté   Asparagus Quiche
Crispbread

Main Courses

Chestnut Pie   Steamed Nutmeat
Walnut Balls   Red Wine and Sage Sauce
Red Wine and Sage Sauce   Bircher Potatoes
Bircher Potatoes   Sprouts with Chestnuts
Parsnips in Yogurt   Cauliflower Amandine
Sprouts with Chestnuts

Desserts

Mincemeat and   Christmas Pudding
Apple Crumble   Brandy Butter
Cream   Cream
                            Mincepies

A. Starters

AVOCADO PÂTÉ

Imperial (Metric)
6 avocados
¼ pint (150ml) olive oil
1 medium onion, chopped very finely
Sea salt
Juice of 2 lemons
2 red chillis
Red pepper to garnish

American
6 avocados
⅔ cupful olive oil
1 medium onion, chopped very finely
Sea salt
Juice of 2 lemons
2 red chillis
Red pepper to garnish

1. Blend all the ingredients except the red pepper.

2. Decorate with red pepper strips.

ASPARAGUS QUICHE

Imperial (Metric)
¾ lb (350g) shortcrust pastry
 (page 88)
3½ oz (90g) asparagus tips (drained
 weight)
4 eggs
4 tablespoonsful double cream
2 tablespoonsful Cheddar cheese,
 grated
3 tablespoonsful juice from
 asparagus tin
Black pepper

American
12 ounces shortcrust pastry
 (page 88)
3½ ounces asparagus tips (drained
 weight)
4 eggs
4 tablespoonsful heavy cream
2 tablespoonsful Cheddar cheese,
 grated
3 tablespoonsful juice from
 asparagus can
Black pepper

1. Roll out the pastry and line a large flan case. Place greaseproof paper and a handful of soya beans on top and bake blind at 400°F/200°C (Gas Mark 6) for about 12 minutes.

2. Remove the greaseproof paper and beans and place the asparagus attractively in the flan case with tips toward the centre.

3. Whisk together the eggs, cream, cheese and asparagus juice and pour carefully over the asparagus.

4. Grind a little black pepper (or nutmeg) over the top of the quiche and bake at 350°F/180°C (Gas Mark 4) for 30 minutes or so until brown on top.

B. Main Courses

CHESTNUT PIE

Imperial (Metric)
¾ lb (350g) shortcrust pastry
  (page 88)
1 medium onion, finely chopped
1 clove garlic
2 tablespoonsful vegetable oil
4 oz (100g) mushrooms, sliced
15½ oz (440g) tin chestnut *purée*
1 tablespoonful brandy
1 egg
1 teaspoonful basil
Seasoning

American
12 ounces shortcrust pastry
  (page 88)
1 medium onion, finely chopped
1 clove garlic
2 tablespoonsful vegetable oil
2 cupsful mushrooms, sliced
1 medium can chestnut paste
1 tablespoonful brandy
1 egg
1 teaspoonful basil
Seasoning

1. Roll out two-thirds of the pastry to a rectangular shape and line a baking tin. Roll out the rest to make the top.

2. Fry the onions and garlic in the oil until transparent.

3. Add the mushrooms and fry for 5 minutes longer.

4. Add the onion mix to the chestnuts and mix well. Stir in the brandy, egg, herbs and seasoning.

5. Fill the pastry case with the chestnut mix.

6. Put the top of the pie into place, seal the edges and make a small hole in the centre to release the steam.

7. Bake for 50 minutes at 350°F/180°C (Gas Mark 4).

STEAMED NUTMEAT

Imperial (Metric)	American
4 oz (100g) polyunsaturated margarine	½ cupful polyunsaturated margarine
4 oz (100g) soya flour	1 cupful soya flour
4 oz (100g) ground almonds	1 cupful ground almonds
4 tablespoonsful soya sauce	4 tablespoonsful soya sauce
3 tablespoonsful herbs	3 tablespoonsful herbs
15½ oz (440g) tin chestnut *purée*	1 medium can chestnut paste
¾ lb (350g) ground walnuts	3 cupsful ground English walnuts

1. Mix all the ingredients together until smooth. If too soft, add more soya flour.

2. Put into a greased bowl and steam for 2 hours or more.

WALNUT BALLS

Imperial (Metric)	American
6 oz (150g) walnuts, ground	1½ cupsful English walnuts, ground
3 oz (75g) breadcrumbs	1½ cupsful breadcrumbs
4 oz (100g) Cheddar cheese, grated	1 cupful Cheddar cheese, grated
1 medium onion, grated	1 medium onion, grated
Pepper	Pepper
Sea salt	Sea salt
2 tablespoonsful parsley	2 tablespoonsful parsley
1 tin red peppers, diced	1 can red peppers, diced
1 egg, beaten	1 egg, beaten
Milk (if required)	Milk (if required)

1. Mix the walnuts, breadcrumbs, cheese and onion in a bowl.

2. Season with salt and pepper and add the parsley and red pepper.

3. Finally, add the egg and combine well with the other ingredients. If the mixture is too dry, add a little milk.

4. Form the mixture into balls and arrange in a well-greased baking dish.

5. Bake in a moderate oven at 350°F/180°C (Gas Mark 4) for about 25 minutes until brown.

RED WINE AND SAGE SAUCE

Imperial (Metric)	American
1 pint (½ litre) vegetable stock	2½ cupsful vegetable stock
1 medium onion	1 medium onion
1 tablespoonful dried sage	1 tablespoonful dried sage
3 bay leaves	3 bay leaves
1 pint (½ litre) red wine	2½ cupsful red wine
3 tablespoonsful vegetable oil	3 tablespoonsful vegetable oil
2 oz (50g) wholemeal flour	½ cupful wholewheat flour
1 teaspoonful sea salt	1 teaspoonful sea salt
2 tablespoonsful lemon juice	2 tablespoonsful lemon juice
1 tablespoonful raw cane sugar	1 tablespoonful raw cane sugar

1. Boil together the stock, onion, sage, bay leaves and wine until reduced by half and strain.

2. Heat the oil, work in the flour and gradually add the strained liquid.

3. Boil the sauce and add salt, sugar and lemon juice.

BIRCHER POTATOES

Imperial (Metric)	American
6 medium potatoes, cleaned but not peeled	6 medium potatoes, cleaned but not peeled
2 oz (50g) vegetable fat	5 tablespoonsful vegetable fat
1 teaspoonful caraway seeds	1 teaspoonful caraway seeds
½ teaspoonful sea salt	½ teaspoonful sea salt

1. Slice each potato into two equal halves.

2. Melt the fat in a baking tray and sprinkle in the caraway seeds and salt.

3. Place the potatoes flat-side down into the baking tray and bake at 350°F/180°C (Gas Mark 4) for an hour until brown on the cut side.

Note: Cumin seeds can be used instead of caraway seeds.

PARSNIPS IN YOGURT

Imperial (Metric)	American
2 lb (1 kilo) parsnips, sliced and parboiled	2 pounds parsnips, sliced and parboiled
3 oz (75g) polyunsaturated margarine	⅓ cupful polyunsaturated margarine
2 tablespoonsful wholemeal flour	2 tablespoonsful wholewheat flour
½ teaspoonful sea salt	½ teaspoonful sea salt
1 pint (½ litre) yogurt	1½ cupsful yogurt
Juice of 2 lemons	Juice of 2 lemons

1. Peel the parsnips and parboil for 10 minutes.

2. Slice into a greased oven dish.

3. Blend the margarine and flour and add the other ingredients and pour over the parsnips.

4. Bake at 350°F/180°C (Gas Mark 4) until tender (about 45 minutes).

SPROUTS WITH CHESTNUTS

Imperial (Metric)	American
½ lb (¼ kilo) fresh chestnuts	8 ounces fresh chestnuts
1½ lb (¾ kilo) Brussels sprouts	1½ pounds Brussels sprouts
2 oz (50g) butter	5 tablespoonsful butter
1 medium onion, finely chopped	1 medium onion, finely chopped
Sea salt	Sea salt

1. Peel the chestnuts by first slitting and placing in boiling water. Boil for 10 minutes until just tender.

2. Remove the outer leaves and ends of stems of the sprouts. Slit the stems to a depth of ½ in. (1cm).

3. Bring a pan of slightly salted water to the boil and boil the sprouts for about 8 minutes — they should not be over soft.

4. Melt the butter and fry the onion for 2 minutes.

5. Add the chestnuts and stir for another minute.

6. Mix the chestnuts in with the sprouts.

Note: Dried chestnuts or tinned chestnuts can be used in this dish.

CAULIFLOWER AMANDINE

Imperial (Metric)	American
1 cauliflower	1 cauliflower
4 oz (100g) butter	½ cupful butter
Sea salt	Sea salt
Pepper	Pepper
2 oz (50g) almonds, blanched and halved	½ cupful almonds, blanched and halved
2 tablespoonsful lemon juice	2 tablespoonsful lemon juice

1. Break the cauliflower into florets and immerse in boiling water for 5 minutes or so and then drain.

2. Melt the butter in a pan and lightly brown the almonds over a low heat then stir in the salt, lemon juice and pepper.

3. Pour the almond and butter mixture over the cauliflower and serve hot.

CHRISTMAS PUDDING
Makes two puddings

Imperial (Metric)	American
½ lb (¼ kilo) currants	1⅓ cupsful currants
½ lb (¼ kilo) sultanas	1⅓ cupsful golden seedless raisins
½ lb (¼ kilo) raisins	1⅓ cupsful raisins
4 oz (100g) apricots, chopped	⅔ cupful apricots, chopped
Grated peel and juice from 1 orange	Grated peel and juice from 1 orange
Grated peel and juice from 1 lemon	Grated peel and juice from 1 lemon
3 eggs, beaten	3 eggs, beaten
½ lb (¼ kilo) cooking apples, grated	1⅓ cupsful cooking apples, grated
6 oz (150g) wholemeal flour	1½ cupsful wholewheat flour
½ lb (¼ kilo) wholemeal breadcrumbs	4 cupsful wholewheat breadcrumbs
4 oz (100g) vegetable fat, grated	½ cupful vegetable fat, grated
1 teaspoonful cinnamon	1 teaspoonful cinnamon
1 teaspoonful nutmeg, grated	1 teaspoonful nutmeg, grated
1 tablespoonful molasses	1 tablespoonful molasses
2 tablespoonsful brandy	2 tablespoonsful brandy

1. Mix all the dried fruits, peel, flour and breadcrumbs.

2. Mix in the vegetable fat, grated apple, spice and molasses.

3. Mix in the eggs, lemon and orange juice and brandy.

4. When the pudding has been well mixed put it into 2 basins and cover with greaseproof paper. Tie securely.

5. Steam for 6 to 8 hours.

BRANDY BUTTER

Imperial (Metric)	American
4 oz (100g) unsalted butter	½ cupful unsalted butter
4 oz (100g) soft raw cane sugar	⅔ cupful soft raw cane sugar
3 tablespoonsful brandy	3 tablespoonsful brandy

1. Beat the butter until softened and add the sugar gradually.

2. Beat in the brandy gradually and, when well mixed, chill until serving.

Note: Rum can be substituted for the brandy if you prefer.

MINCEMEAT AND APPLE CRUMBLE

For the Mincemeat:

Imperial (Metric)	American
½ lb (¼ kilo) raisins	1⅓ cupsful raisins
1 lb (½ kilo) sultanas	2⅔ cupsful golden seedless raisins
½ lb (¼ kilo) cooking apples	8 ounces cooking apples
½ lb (¼ kilo) Brazil nuts	1½ cupsful Brazil nuts
½ lb (¼ kilo) vegetable fat	1 cupful vegetable fat
1 lb (½ kilo) currants	2⅔ cupsful currants
Grated peel and juice from 2 lemons	Grated peel and juice from 2 lemons
Grated peel and juice from 2 oranges	Grated peel and juice from 2 oranges
1 teaspoonful nutmeg	1 teaspoonful nutmeg
2 tablespoonsful brandy	2 tablespoonsful brandy

1. Mince the raisins and sultanas.

2. Grate the apples, Brazils and fat.

3. Combine all the ingredients and mix well.

4. Keep in the refrigerator until required.

For the Crumble:

Imperial (Metric)	American
1 lb (½ kilo) apples, peeled and sliced	1 pound apples, peeled and sliced
½ lb (¼ kilo) mincemeat	8 ounces mincemeat
½ teaspoonful cinnamon powder	½ teaspoonful cinnamon powder
6 oz (150g) wholemeal flour	1½ cupsful wholewheat flour
4 oz (100g) polyunsaturated margarine	½ cupful polyunsaturated margarine
1 tablespoonful oatflakes (optional)	1 tablespoonful oatflakes (optional)

1. Slice the apples into a casserole dish and sprinkle with cinnamon.

2. Spread mincemeat evenly over the apples.

3. Mix the flour and margarine and spread over the mincemeat. Top with flaked oats if you wish.

4. Bake at 350°F/180°C (Gas Mark 4) for 30 minutes until brown.

MINCE PIES

Imperial (Metric)	American
¾ lb (350g) shortcrust pastry (page 88)	12 ounces shortcrust pastry (page 88)
½ lb (¼ kilo) mincemeat	8 ounces mincemeat
2 teaspoonsful raw cane sugar	2 teaspoonsful raw cane sugar

1. Roll out the pastry thinly and line mince-pie tins. Add the mincemeat and cover with pastry.

2. Seal carefully and sprinkle a little sugar on the top of each.

3. Bake at 400°F/200°C (Gas Mark 6) for 20 minutes.

11.

OUTDOOR MEALS

There are few more pleasurable occasions than a meal eaten in the open air on a fine summer's day in a picturesque setting. A little more preparation and forethought is required than for a meal in your own home, as you must avoid settling in a field after a longish walk only to find that you have forgotten to bring any cutlery or a corkscrew.

Amongst the dishes that could be chosen from other chapters for an outdoor party, are Scotch Eggs (page 155), Walnut Balls (page 164), Tarte a l'Oignon Alsacienne (page 90), Turkish Pilaff (page 108), Mushrooms in Olive Oil (page 79) and three salads (pages 188-189).

If you can find a spot near to a running stream, you will be able to keep the wine or other drink cool. You should take a covering for the ground such as a large blanket, and a table cloth, on which to lay out the food. Make sure that where it lies is flat and solid.

An excellent starter is a cold soup such as Gazpacho, which can be transported in a flask and served in disposable bowls with wholemeal rolls and butter. If you decide on a pâté chosen from Chapter 6, 8, or 10, you must keep it cool at all times, but as long as this is possible, a pâté would be a suitable alternative to Gazpacho.

A creamy Mushroom Quiche will be enjoyed by all who partake but is a little awkward to transport. Generous use of cling-film will ease this problem and a board placed on the flan dish will mean that other articles can be packed on top.

Chestnut pasties are always a favourite at outdoor functions which I attend, though other fillings are possible. If the pasties are individually wrapped in cling-film soon after being cooked (but when cool) they can be carried in a bag, box or plastic container.

It is possible to purchase a burger press obviously designed for making beef and hamburgers but which is equally useful for making neatly shaped vegetarian burgers from nutmixes as described in Chapter 10. The recipe here is for aptly named Sunburgers, making use of sunflower seeds. If they are wrapped individually, similar to the pasties, they are equally convenient to transport.

The salads are a necessary complement to the savoury dishes and all show how fruit can be used successfully alongside savoury ingredients. These include pineapple in a Rice Salad, apricots in a Potato Salad, banana and sultanas with carrot and strawberries in a Mixed Salad. You should choose three of these salads depending on the availability of ingredients.

If you have no plans to move from your idyllic spot until after a rest in the sun, you could indulge in a final course of Stilton and port.

As a drink to accompany the main course, I would take a choice of a light white wine and a red such as Riesling and Beaujolais respectively.

I have included a list of items that you will need on your picnic. Cutlery and crockery may be of a disposable variety and this will be lighter to carry and avoid breakages, the chance of which is high on this sort of occasion.

The salads can be served in the containers in which they are transported, so whether you decide to take serving dishes as well will depend on the grandeur of the occasion and the strength of the participants to carry them.

SUGGESTED MENU
for 6 people

Starters
Gazpacho
Wholemeal Rolls and Butter

Main Courses
Mushroom Quiche (or Chestnut Pasties)
Sunburgers
Summer Rice Salad
Potato Salad
Mixed Salad with Strawberries
(or Carrot and Banana Salad)

Desserts
Stilton
Red Apples

Items to Remember
Blanket or Groundsheet
Bowls
Corkscrew
Cutlery
Glasses
Kitchen Paper
Plates
Serviettes
Serving Spoons
Tablecloth
Waste Bin Liner

A. Starter

GAZPACHO

Imperial (Metric)
4 slices wholemeal bread, cubed
2 cloves garlic
1 teaspoonful sea salt
4 tablespoonsful lemon juice
½ pint (¼ litre) water
½ cucumber, diced
1 green pepper, chopped
1 medium onion, chopped
2 lb (1 kilo) tomatoes, quartered
½ pint (¼ litre) olive oil

American
4 slices wholewheat bread, cubed
2 cloves garlic
1 teaspoonful sea salt
4 tablespoonsful lemon juice
1⅓ cupsful water
½ cucumber, diced
1 green pepper, chopped
1 medium onion, chopped
2 pounds tomatoes, quartered
1⅓ cupsful olive oil

1. Combine all the ingredients except the oil and liquidize until smooth.

2. Add the oil gradually and combine with the Gazpacho to make a creamy mixture.

3. Taste and adjust the seasoning.

4. Chill and transport in a flask.

B. Main Courses

MUSHROOM QUICHE

Imperial (Metric)
¾ lb (350g) shortcrust pastry
  (page 88)
¾ lb (350g) mushrooms, sliced
1 oz (25g) butter
¼ pint (150ml) single cream
4 eggs
Sea salt
Black pepper
2 tablespoonsful Cheddar cheese,
  grated

American
12 ounces shortcrust pastry
  (page 88)
6 cupsful mushrooms, sliced
2½ tablespoonsful butter
⅔ cupful light cream
4 eggs
Sea salt
Black pepper
2 tablespoonsful Cheddar cheese,
  grated

1. Roll out the pastry and line a large flan dish. Place greaseproof paper and a few beans on the pastry case and bake blind at 400°F/200°C (Gas Mark 6) for about 12 minutes.

2. Cook the sliced mushrooms gently in the butter for 10 minutes.

3. Arrange the mushrooms evenly in the flan case.

4. Combine the cream and eggs and a little salt and blend well.

5. Pour the egg and cream mixture on the mushrooms and sprinkle cheese on the top. Finally mill a little black pepper over the quiche.

6. Bake at 350°F/180°C (Gas Mark 4) for 30 minutes until brown on top.

CHESTNUT PASTIES

Imperial (Metric)
¾ lb (350g) shortcrust pastry
  (page 88)
Vegetable oil
2 medium onions, finely chopped
1 tablespoonful basil
3 tablespoonsful tomato *purée*
15½ oz (440g) tin chestnut *purée*
1 egg, beaten, to glaze (optional)

American
12 ounces shortcrust pastry
  (page 88)
Vegetable oil
2 medium onions, finely chopped
1 tablespoonful basil
3 tablespoonsful tomato paste
1 medium can chestnut paste
1 egg, beaten, to glaze (optional)

1. Roll out the pastry and use a saucepan lid with about a 7 in. (17cm) diameter to cut out circles, each of which will make one pasty (make smaller ones if you wish).

2. Heat a little oil and fry the onion until transparent.

3. Add the basil and tomato *purée* and mix with the onion.

4. Add the chestnut *purée* and mix in or mash with the other ingredients. Allow to cool slightly before using.

5. Put a tablespoonful of the chestnut mixture into the middle of each pastry circle and dampen the edges to be sealed with a pastry brush.

6. Bring the edges together and seal. With the sealed edge uppermost, put a gentle wave into the sealed edge by pushing the pastry one way and the other alternately as your fingers move along it.

7. Glaze with beaten egg if you wish.

8. Bake at 350°F/180°C (Gas Mark 4) for about 30 minutes.

SUNBURGERS

Imperial (Metric)	American
1 medium onion, finely chopped	1 medium onion, finely chopped
Olive oil	Olive oil
10 oz (300g) sunflower seeds, ground	2½ cupsful sunflower seeds, ground
6 oz (150g) carrots, grated	1 cupful carrots, grated
1 tablespoonful dried parsley	1 tablespoonful dried parsley
1 egg	1 egg
Pepper	Pepper
Sea salt	Sea salt
Oatmeal	Oatmeal

1. Fry the onion in a little oil until transparent.

2. Mix together all the ingredients.

3. Form into six burgers, preferably with a burger maker.

4. Coat each burger with oatmeal and fry in oil (preferably olive oil) for about 8 minutes on each side until brown. Alternatively the burgers can be baked in a moderate oven for 20 minutes.

CARROT AND BANANA SALAD

Imperial (Metric)	American
2 bananas	2 bananas
¾ lb (350g) carrots, grated	2 cupsful carrots, grated
6 oz (150g) sultanas	1 cupful golden seedless raisins
4 tablespoonsful lemon juice	4 tablespoonsful lemon juice
2 oz (50g) almonds, blanched and flaked	½ cupful almonds, blanched and slivered
Parsley	Parsley

1. Slice the bananas evenly.

2. Combine all the ingredients and serve garnished with parsley.

SUMMER RICE SALAD

Imperial (Metric)	American
1 avocado	1 avocado
2 tablespoonsful lemon juice	2 tablespoonsful lemon juice
½ lb (¼ kilo) long-grain brown rice, cooked	1⅓ cupsful long-grain brown rice, cooked
½ lb (¼ kilo) pineapple pieces	½ pound pineapple pieces
3 tablespoonsful cashew nuts	3 tablespoonsful cashew nuts
6 spring onions, finely chopped	6 scallions, finely chopped
1 tablespoonful cider vinegar	1 tablespoonful cider vinegar
2 tablespoonsful olive oil	2 tablespoonsful olive oil
1 clove garlic	1 clove garlic
Sea salt	Sea salt
½ red pepper, thinly sliced	½ red pepper, thinly sliced

1. Peel the avocado and dice the flesh. Pour 1 tablespoonful of lemon juice on the avocado flesh to prevent its discoloration.

2. Combine the rice, avocado, pineapple, cashews and spring onions (scallions).

3. In a blender put 1 tablespoonful of lemon juice, the cider vinegar, olive oil, garlic and seasoning. Blend until smooth.

4. Pour the dressing over the salad.

5. Arrange red pepper slices over the top of the salad.

POTATO SALAD WITH APRICOTS AND WALNUTS

Imperial (Metric)
1 lb (½ kilo) new potatoes, cleaned
Sea salt
Pepper
6 tablespoonsful mayonnaise
12 dried apricots, halved lengthwise
3 oz (75g) walnuts (large pieces)
2 tablespoonsful chives or spring onion tops

American
1 pound new potatoes, cleaned
Sea salt
Pepper
6 tablespoonsful mayonnaise
12 dried apricots, halved lengthwise
⅔ cupful English walnuts (large pieces)
2 tablespoonsful chives or scallion tops

1. Boil the potatoes until tender and dice into convenient sized pieces.

2. When the potatoes have cooled, season and combine with the mayonnaise and apricots.

3. Just before serving mix in the walnuts and half the chives.

4. Sprinkle the remainder of the chives over the top of the salad.

MIXED SALAD WITH STRAWBERRIES

Imperial (Metric)	American
1 green pepper	1 green pepper
Lettuce, washed and drained	Lettuce, washed and drained
1 bunch watercress, washed and drained	1 bunch watercress, washed and drained
½ cucumber, thinly sliced	½ cucumber, thinly sliced
4 tomatoes, sliced	4 tomatoes, sliced
8 radishes, sliced	8 radishes, sliced
½ lb (¼ kilo) strawberries, washed	½ pound strawberries, washed

For the Dressing:

Imperial (Metric)	American
1 tablespoonful lemon juice	1 tablespoonful lemon juice
1 tablespoonful cider vinegar	1 tablespoonful cider vinegar
1 tablespoonful wholegrain mustard	1 tablespoonful wholegrain mustard
1 teaspoonful honey	1 teaspoonful honey
4 tablespoonsful olive oil	4 tablespoonsful olive oil
Sea salt	Sea salt
Black pepper	Black pepper

1. Chop the green pepper into small pieces.

2. Tear each lettuce leaf into 3 or 4 pieces.

3. Combine all the ingredients for the salad.

4. Blend the ingredients for the dressing and pour over the salad a few minutes before serving.

12.

FONDUE DINNER PARTY

I have refrained from calling this a Swiss dinner party as not all the
dishes are specifically Swiss, though many have a connection with
Switzerland. Certainly a fondue is a splendid meal because of the
participation of the diners, the superb aroma and flavour of the melted
cheese, and the ways in which the meal can be varied to suit all
occasions. For instance, it is possible to use cider and Cheddar or
Gouda instead of the more expensive white wine and Swiss cheese.
In fact, I have even made fondue with beer and all variations have
been excellent.

You may wish to launch straight into the fondue but both the
Chestnut Soup and the Asparagus with Breadcrumbs are suitable
starters which might be served at a dinner party in Switzerland.
Chestnut soup is unusual outside central Europe, but it should be
tried and will then become an established part of your repertoire of
dishes.

It is possible to serve a fondue without a special fondue set but as
the cheese cools it becomes stringy so a fondue set is a worthwhile
investment and I have even used one successfully outdoors. The fondue
set itself consists of a copper stove part, in which you should use
methylated spirits to give the flame, which can be regulated by a simple
device which restricts the amount of air. The fondue pot is usually
a heavy glazed earthenware vessel.

The fondue itself can be prepared on your stove in a saucepan then
transferred into the fondue pan just before serving. A mat should
be placed in the centre of the table and on it put the burner. When
the fondue pan is brought to the table you should regulate the flame

so that the fondue continues to boil gently. Have a variety of items to dip into the fondue besides the usual cubes of wholemeal bread; I have suggested Button Mushrooms and Potato Balls here but you may be able to think of other alternatives. Bread or other items should be placed on the special fondue fork and it may be left to rest in the fondue pot while you eat some salad or sip your wine. It is worth noting, however, that it is a Swiss custom that if any lady should drop her piece of bread in the fondue she should kiss all the men present, while if a man should lose his bread he should buy a round of kirsch. You could probably devise even better forfeits than these!

I generally use a Niersteiner wine in making the fondue and to accompany it, but a Swiss Fondant or Neuchatel is preferable if it can be obtained. A couple of salads should be served with the fondue so choose from the three given or any salad with a number of crisp, crunchy ingredients.

You may decide that no dessert is necessary after such a feast, but the Swiss Apple Pie will prove an interesting variation on crumble. Moreover, baking it in a pastry case will enable you to cut it out in neat pieces.

SUGGESTED MENU

Starters
Chestnut Soup (or Asparagus with Breadcrumbs)

Main Course
Swiss Cheese Fondue
Cubed Wholemeal Bread
Button Mushrooms
Potato Balls
Waldorf Salad (or Cauliflower Salad)
Green Salad

Dessert
Swiss Apple Pie

A. Starters

CHESTNUT SOUP

Imperial (Metric)	American
1 oz (25g) butter	2½ tablespoonsful butter
2 tablespoonsful wholemeal flour	2 tablespoonsful wholewheat flour
1 pint (½ litre) vegetable stock	2½ cupsful vegetable stock
15½ oz (440g) tin chestnut *purée*	1 medium can chestnut paste
4 tablespoonsful red wine	4 tablespoonsful red wine
1 tablespoonful brandy	1 tablespoonful brandy
Sea salt	Sea salt
Pepper	Pepper
Paprika	Paprika

1. Melt the butter and mix in the flour for a minute or so.

2. Slowly add the stock, then the chestnuts.

3. Add the wine, brandy and season with salt and pepper.

4. Blend well and simmer gently for 20 minutes.

5. Sprinkle with paprika before serving.

ASPARAGUS WITH BREADCRUMBS

Imperial (Metric)	**American**
1 tin asparagus tips	1 can asparagus tips
Nutmeg, grated	Nutmeg, grated
1 oz (25g) butter	2½ tablespoonsful butter
4 oz (100g) wholemeal breadcrumbs	2 cupsful wholewheat breadcrumbs

1. Lay the asparagus in a serving dish and scatter a little nutmeg over them.

2. Place under a low grill or in a moderate oven for a short time. Use a little juice from the tin to prevent them drying up.

3. Melt the butter in a pan and stir in the breadcrumbs for 2 minutes.

4. Sprinkle the breadcrumbs over the asparagus and place under the grill until fairly crisp.

B. Main Course

SWISS CHEESE FONDUE

Imperial (Metric)	**American**
Up to ¾ pint (400ml) white wine	2 cupsful white wine
14 oz (400g) Gruyère cheese, grated	3½ cupsful Gruyère cheese, grated
7 oz (200g) Emmenthal cheese, grated	1¾ cupsful Emmenthal cheese, grated
1 clove garlic	1 clove garlic
2 tablespoonsful kirsch	2 tablespoonsful kirsch
1½ tablespoonsful arrowroot	1½ tablespoonsful arrowroot
1 tablespoonful lemon juice	1 tablespoonful lemon juice
Nutmeg, grated	Nutmeg, grated
Pepper	Pepper

For Dipping:

Imperial (Metric)	American
Cubed wholemeal bread	Cubed wholewheat bread
1 lb (½ kilo) button mushrooms (fried in butter until tender)	8 cupsful button mushrooms (fried in butter until tender)
Potato balls (below)	Potato balls (below)

1. Rub the fondue pot well with garlic.

2. Heat the wine in a saucepan and gradually sprinkle into it the cheese, stirring constantly.

3. Mix the kirsch with the arrowroot and lemon juice and pour into the cheese and wine mixture.

4. Season with pepper and a little grated nutmeg.

POTATO BALLS

Imperial (Metric)	American
1 lb (½ kilo) mashed potato	2½ cupsful mashed potato
2 egg yolks	2 egg yolks
2 tablespoonsful wholemeal flour	2 tablespoonsful wholewheat flour
Sea salt	Sea salt
3 tablespoonsful fine wholemeal breadcrumbs	3 tablespoonsful fine wholewheat breadcrumbs
Vegetable oil for deep-frying	Vegetable oil for deep-frying

1. Mix the mashed potato with most of the egg yolk and flour. Add a little salt.

2. Shape into smallish balls about 1½ in. (3cm) across.

3. Dip each ball in the remaining egg yolk and roll in breadcrumbs.

4. Deep fry in the oil until brown.

WALDORF SALAD

Imperial (Metric)	American
1 head celery	1 head celery
2 lb (900g) red apples	2 pounds red apples
4 oz (100g) dates, chopped	¾ cupful dates, chopped
6 oz (150g) walnuts	1⅓ cupsful English walnuts
6 tablespoonsful mayonnaise	6 tablespoonsful mayonnaise
6 lettuce leaves	6 lettuce leaves
Paprika	Paprika

1. Wash the celery and chop each stalk diagonally into ½ in. (1cm) pieces.

2. Wash and core the apples. Slice each quarter into about 8 pieces.

3. Mix the apple, celery, dates and half the walnuts with the mayonnaise and pile onto a bed of lettuce leaves.

4. Place a few large walnut pieces on top of the salad and dust with paprika.

CAULIFLOWER SALAD

Imperial (Metric)	American
4 oz (100g) sultanas	⅔ cupful golden seedless raisins
2 tablespoonsful lemon juice	2 tablespoonsful lemon juice
1 cauliflower, washed and grated	1 cauliflower, washed and grated
2 tablespoonsful mayonnaise	2 tablespoonsful mayonnaise
3 tablespoonsful yogurt	3 tablespoonsful yogurt
4 oz (100g) walnuts	¾ cupful English walnuts
6 lettuce leaves	6 lettuce leaves
½ teaspoonful mint	½ teaspoonful mint

1. Soak the sultanas (golden seedless raisins) in the lemon juice for an hour or so.

2. Mix the grated cauliflower with the sultanas (golden seedless raisins), mayonnaise and yogurt. Mix in half the walnuts as well.

3. Pile onto a bed of lettuce.

4. Place a few walnut pieces on the top and sprinkle chopped mint over the salad.

GREEN SALAD

Imperial (Metric)	American
1 lettuce, washed and drained	1 lettuce, washed and drained
1 head chicory, trimmed	1 head chicory, trimmed
1 bunch watercress, washed and drained	1 bunch watercress, washed and drained
6 spring onions, cleaned	6 scallions, cleaned
½ cucumber	½ cucumber
1 green pepper	1 green pepper

Dressing:

Imperial (Metric)	American
2 tablespoonsful lemon juice	2 tablespoonsful lemon juice
2 tablespoonsful cider vinegar	2 tablespoonsful cider vinegar
1 tablespoonful wholegrain mustard	1 tablespoonful wholegrain mustard
1 clove garlic	1 clove garlic
1 tablespoonful raw cane sugar	1 tablespoonful raw cane sugar
5 tablespoonsful olive oil	5 tablespoonsful olive oil
Sea salt	Sea salt
Pepper	Pepper

1. Tear the lettuce leaves into 3 or 4 pieces.

2. Slice the chicory.

3. Halve the spring onions (scallions) lengthways. If they are thick ones, quarter them.

4. Slice the cucumber and green pepper thinly.

5. Mix the salad items together well.

6. Blend the dressing and pour over the salad just before serving.

C. Dessert

SWISS APPLE PIE

Imperial (Metric)	American
¾ lb (350g) shortcrust pastry (page 88)	12 ounces shortcrust pastry (page 88)
¾ lb (350g) apple *purée*	2 cupsful apple paste
1 teaspoonful cinnamon, ground	1 teaspoonful cinnamon, ground
2 tablespoonsful sultanas	2 tablespoonsful golden seedless
4 oz (100g) rolled oats	raisins
2 oz (50g) polyunsaturated margarine	1 cupful rolled oats
1 tablespoonful raw cane sugar	¼ cupful polyunsaturated margarine
	1 tablespoonful raw cane sugar

1. Line a large flan dish with the pastry, cover with greaseproof paper and a few beans. Bake blind at 400°F/200°C (Gas Mark 6) for 10 minutes.

2. Spread in the apple pulp which should be fairly dry.

3. Sprinkle over the cinnamon and sultanas (golden seedless raisins).

4. Mix the rolled oats, margarine and sugar.

5. Spread this mixture over the apple.

6. Bake at 350°F/180°C (Gas Mark 4) for 20 minutes.

INDEX